Michael Drayton, Samuel Daniel, Henry Charles Beeching

A Selection from the Poetry of Samuel Daniel & Michael Drayton

Michael Drayton, Samuel Daniel, Henry Charles Beeching
A Selection from the Poetry of Samuel Daniel & Michael Drayton
ISBN/EAN: 9783337176372
Printed in Europe, USA, Canada, Australia, Japan
Cover: Foto ©ninafisch / pixelio.de

More available books at **www.hansebooks.com**

Samuel Daniel.

A SELECTION FROM THE POETRY OF SAMUEL DANIEL
&
MICHAEL DRAYTON

With an Introduction and Notes by
The Rev. H. C. Beeching, M.A.

LONDON
J. M. DENT & CO.
29 AND 30 BEDFORD STREET
1899

TO

MY OXFORD PUPILS

CONTENTS

	PAGE
INTRODUCTION	ix

A SELECTION FROM THE POEMS OF SAMUEL DANIEL

Sonnets to Delia	1
From the Complaint of Rosamond	16
From the Tragedy of Cleopatra	20
From the Civil Wars	27
Epistle to the Lady Margaret, Countess of Cumberland	33
From Musophilus	38
From the Epistle to Sir Thomas Egerton	41
From the Tragedy of Philotas	44
Ulysses and the Siren	46
From the Queen's Arcadia	49
From Tethys' Festival	50
From Hymen's Triumph	51
An Ode	55

A SELECTION FROM THE POEMS OF MICHAEL DRAYTON

Daffadill	57
From Endymion and Phœbe	60

Contents

	PAGE
From England's Heroical Epistles	62
The Tower of Mortimer—From the Baron's Wars	69
Idea (Sonnets)	77
To the New Year	88
To His Valentine	92
The Heart	95
To Master John Savage	97
The Crier	99
To his Coy Love	100
To his Rival	101
Ballad of Agincourt	103
To the Virginian Voyage	107
An Ode Written in the Peak	110
From Poly-Olbion (Milford Haven)	112
,, (Guy of Warwick)	114
An Elegy	118
Nymphidia—The Court of Fairy	125
The Shepherd's Sirena	148
From the Muses' Elysium	160
,, The Second Nymphal	165
,, The Sixth Nymphal	176

INTRODUCTION

IF any apology be required for bringing within the covers of a single volume a selection from both Daniel and Drayton, it must be offered in the circumstance that occasioned it. Having to lecture for the Oxford School of Literature upon the minor Elizabethan poets, I could find no text of either Daniel or Drayton to put into my pupils' hands. Of Drayton indeed Mr A. H. Bullen issued an excellent selection in 1883, but his book is now as scarce as the early copies, and almost as expensive. The only other modern texts I know are Hooper's reprint of the *Poly-Olbion*, and Morley's of the *Barons' Wars* and a few other pieces, a useful book, but neither representative nor discriminating enough for my purpose. Of Daniel there has been no edition[1] since the two little volumes of 1718, and no selection but that of Mr John Morris in 1855 issued to subscribers at Bath. Under these circumstances, Mr Dent generously came to my help, and consented to publish a small book containing the choice poems of both writers.

The association of the two is thus avowedly fortuitous, but it will not, I venture to think, be

[1] Dr Grosart in 1885 issued an edition of 150 copies for private circulation, in which an attempt was made to collate texts. But the notes at the end of this volume will make clear that a satisfactory collation is still wanting.

found unreasonable or without a special interest. They were contemporaries, born within a year of each other, and both reflect, with characteristic peculiarities, the influences to which poetry was subject at the end of the sixteenth century. A glance at the table which follows this introduction will show that in 1592-3 they were both writing sonnets; a little later they were both writing "Legends," on the model set by the *Mirror for Magistrates*, Daniel taking the story of *Fair Rosamond*, and Drayton those of *Piers Gaveston* and *Matilda the Chaste*. Later again both succumbed to the impulse to write Chronicle History, Daniel choosing the *Wars of the Roses*, and Drayton the *Wars of the Barons under Edward II*. After this the parallel, though it continues, is less close. Both wrote plays, but while Drayton, in an unexplained period of poverty at the end of Elizabeth's reign, became a stage hack, Daniel, under the patronage of the Herberts, wrote classical tragedies, with chorus, in the manner of Seneca. Both again had a taste for pastoral; but Daniel, who held a post at Court, wrote stately masks for the Queen; while Drayton, after experimenting in the style of the *Shepheards Calender*, broke away from convention altogether and wrote what are perhaps the only genuine pastorals in the language. Finally we may note that both wrote verse epistles to their contemporaries; and if Daniel compiled a History of England in prose, Drayton wrote a Geography of England— the *Poly-Olbion*—in what cannot, without stretching the term, be called poetry.

To the general reader, Daniel, if he is known

Introduction

at all, is known by his Sonnets. But his Sonnets are not his most distinguishing productions. They are written in good language and correct metre, and the sonnet rhythm—as the Elizabethans understood it—is well preserved. Also they usually open well, *e.g.* "Still in the trace of one perplexed thought," and it is perhaps due to this fact that they are occasionally mentioned in the same sentence with Shakespeare's. Perhaps a few like "And yet I cannot reprehend the flight," or "Look, Delia, how we esteem the half-blown rose," or, "Let others sing of knights and paladins," might indeed pass muster in the second Shakespearean rank. But for the most part the thought is commonplace—a criticism that cannot be made on anything Daniel wrote later, and the excellence is the excellence of single lines, like the address to Apollo:

"O clear-eyed Rector of the holy hill!"

or the description of Delia as

"A modest maid decked with a blush of honour,
Whose feet do tread green paths of youth and love";

or the forecast of old age as a time

"When thou, surcharged with burden of thy years,
Shall bend thy wrinkles homeward to the earth."

When Daniel published in the same volume his *Sonnets to Delia* and his *Complaint of Rosamond*, Spenser gave the book a warm welcome, but hinted that the new poet's strength lay in the "tragical" rather than the amatory poems.[1] The modern reader, even if he must judge from the few extracts here given, is likely to agree with

[1] See the passage in *Colin Clout's come home again*.

Spenser. The poet seems to have had no love affair of his own to draw upon in the sonnets, while in the Rosamond there was at any rate a real experience to rouse his passion.

When we turn from Daniel's sonnets to Drayton's, two points at once strike us. Drayton's are less finished, and the images he employs are apt to be more conventional; but, on the other hand, there is evident in many of them the warmth of a real affection. The splendid sonnet that some critics would fain steal for Shakespeare, "Since there's no help, come, let us kiss and part," reads like all Drayton's later work, as though struck out at a heat. It is as admirable as it is, not from any subtlety of thought or expression, but because it is the simple and passionate rendering of a sincere and passionate mood. It is interesting to know that Drayton began sonneteering as a disciple of Daniel, and then broke away into his freer style, suppressing in 1605 the greater number of the sonnets he had published in 1594. The contrast between the two styles will be plain if the reader will compare in this collection the preciosity of the first and eighth sonnets,

> "Where nightingales in Arden sit and sing
> Among the dainty dew-empearled flowers,"

with the almost blunt simplicity of the rest. These later sonnets usually treat with great freedom and vigour a single idea.[1] More than usually successful

---

[1] In printing the sonnets in this volume I have followed the form of the early copies. Daniel prints in quatrains, Drayton marks no division till the final couplet. The arrangement in each case seems characteristic; or at least it may be regarded as symbolical.

Introduction

examples are those to Humour (p. 81) and to Proverb (p. 86). But it is only on the rare occasions when the idea is itself passionate that they give the reader much delight. Then the passion is certainly heightened by the apparent spontaneity and lack of fastidiousness in the expression; as in the "Dear, why should you command me to my rest," and the unequalled, "Since there's no help." Critics are undoubtedly right in recognising that this latter sonnet touches Drayton's high-water mark; but it is blindness not to see that it is as certainly in Drayton's own characteristic manner as its less happy fellows. Whether Drayton had read Shakespeare's sonnets is a question that would be worth discussing. He had undoubtedly read Sidney's, and read them with care.[1]

To pass to the second phase of our poets' literary activity. Daniel's *Complaint of Rosamond* was published in 1592, and his *First four books of the Civil Wars* in 1595; the first was written in seven-line, the latter in eight-line stanzas. Drayton in 1596 issued his *Mortimeriados* in seven-line stanzas, and in 1603 re-issued it in eight-line as *The Barons' Wars*. The connexion of which events would seem to be this, that Drayton was stimulated by the success of Daniel's *Rosamond* to attempt a similar "tragical" theme, and chose the fall of Mortimer, which he wrote in the same metre; a perfectly familiar

[1] In a sonnet prefixed to the edition of 1605 he mentions Sidney, Constable, and Daniel as the masters in the art. See quotation in note to page 122. Collier pointed out that the line in which Drayton professed his own originality, "I am no pickpurse of another's wit," was borrowed from Sidney.

metre known as rime-royal, and admirably adapted for pathetic monologue. When, however, Daniel's historical poem appeared, Drayton, who though less of an original artist than Daniel was an apt scholar, saw at once how much more suitable the eight-line stanza was for historical narrative; and as his *Mortimeriados* inevitably contained a good deal of narrative, he re-wrote it, simplifying the expression throughout and purging it of much of the poetry. It was perhaps not to be expected that in the preface he wrote to account for the change he should refer to Daniel. The passages here selected from the two poems are such as shew each writer at his best. Neither is a good story-teller; Daniel excels in reflective, Drayton in descriptive passages; even when Daniel is most descriptive, there is an undertone of reflection, as when by way of describing the pageants in the London streets to grace Bolingbroke's entry, he says:

> "Approaching near the city he was met
> With all the sumptuous shows joy could devise,
> *Where new desire to please did not forget*
> *To pass the usual pomp of former guise.*"

Drayton is more directly narrative, and his purple patches are frankly purple patches, such as the fine description of Mortimer's Tower (p. 69).

It may be interesting to compare their handling of a similar theme. Take for this purpose the passages where each poet describes the night his dethroned monarch spends after his fall. Thus Daniel upon Richard:

> "To Flint from thence unto a restless bed
> That miserable night he comes conveyed;

Introduction xv

> Poorly provided, poorly followed,
> Uncourted, unrespected, unobeyed :
> Where if uncertain sleep but hovered
> Over the drooping cares that heavy weighed,
> Millions of figures fantasy presents
> Unto that sorrow wakened grief augments.
>
> " His new misfortune makes deluding sleep
> Say 'twas not so, false dreams the truth deny :
> Wherewith he starts ; feels waking cares do creep
> Upon his soul, and give his dream the lie :
> Then sleeps again, and then again as deep
> Deceits of darkness mock his misery :
> *So hard believed was sorrow in her youth,*
> *That he thinks truth was dreams and dreams were truth.*"

With this compare Drayton upon Edward :

> " By night affrighted in his fearful dreams
> Of raging fiends and goblins that he meets,
> *Of falling down from steep rocks into streams,*
> Of death, of burials, and of winding-sheets,
> *Of wandering helpless in far foreign rea[l]ms.*
> *Of strong temptations by seducing sprights,*
> Wherewith awaked, and calling out for aid,
> His hollow voice doth make himself afraid.
>
> Then came the vision of his bloody reign :—
> Marching along with Lancaster's stern ghost,
> Twenty-eight Barons, either hanged or slain," etc.

The passage from Drayton is the more picturesque and clearly defined ; and the italicised lines in the first stanza are finely descriptive ; then with the procession of twenty-eight barons the dream becomes too realistic. Daniel leaves the dreams to the reader's imagination, but produces far more effect by the pendulous movement of the stanza to and fro between sleep and waking, and by the characteristic touch of reflection with which he closes.

Drayton had displayed the fertility, which was one of his most marked characteristics, by following up his *Mortimeriados*[1] by two other tragical legends in the same manner and metre. Then he struck out a new line of his own. Taking a hint from Ovid, he put together a series of England's Heroical Epistles,[2] all written with great rhetorical skill and with occasional flashes of poetical imagination and feeling. They were long popular, and editions were frequent down to the end of the last century. Mr Elton well parallels them, both as to their conspicuous merits and their defects, with Macaulay's Lays.[3] The Heroical Epistles were not Drayton's first attempt in the heroic metre; already in 1595, before writing *Mortimeriados*, he had written a poem in couplets, after the manner of Marlowe, on the subject of Endymion and Phœbe. A short passage from the opening of this poem is given on page 60.

After the publication of the historical poems the paths of the two poets diverge. Each had now developed his own peculiar powers, and they were strikingly different. Daniel's tendency was to meditation. He was an original and subtle thinker, and he exercised himself on great matters. But abstract thought is a dangerous occupation for a poet, because he is apt to speak with his tongue before the fire of his imagination is kindled. Everyone must admire the thought

[1] Drayton's title proves him to have been no Greek scholar, and all his virtues and vices are unclassical. Daniel, on the other hand, is the most Greek of our elder poets.
[2] In this case it would seem that Daniel imitated Drayton. *Englands Heroicall Epistles* were published in 1597. In 1599 appeared Daniel's *A Letter sent from Octavia to her husband Marcus Antonius into Aegypt.*
[3] See his indispensable "Introduction to Michael Drayton," p. 23.

of *Musophilus*, but its greatest admirer must admit that the passages where the thought takes flame are short and far between. There is more sustained vitality in the Epistles, especially in that to the Countess of Cumberland, which was a favourite poem with Wordsworth.[1] But we feel, as we read and admire, that poetry of this sort approaches very near the confines of prose; and lovers of Daniel may also feel that it was not the work to which the Muses had called him. We are inclined to quote to him the lines of Matthew Arnold, whom he not a little resembles, lines that have been quoted against that very unequal poet himself upon his excursions into criticism:

> "Not here, O Apollo,
> Are haunts meet for thee,
> But where Helicon breaks down
> In cliff to the sea."

When Daniel can keep near the springs of Helicon, and forget criticism, his style at once becomes limpid, and his imagination warm and clear. *Hymen's Triumph*—which is Daniel's triumph—is full from first to last of beautiful thought and beautiful writing. In a copy of Daniel's poems in my possession, that once belonged to Wordsworth, I find the following note in his hand:

"This poem of *Hymen's Triumph* is far superior to the *Queen's Arcadia*. The story, it is true, is grossly improbable, but the piece, although sadly injured by the underplot of Montanus, has sufficient unity of interest, and is everywhere scattered over with beautiful touches of passion

[1] See passages quoted in notes, p. 188.

and description written with true simplicity. The language is throughout admirable, though not altogether without conceits, and the sentiments, where they are pleasing themselves, are sometimes unsuited to the characters."

To the passages which will be found quoted in the sequel, one or two shorter pieces may be added here, as the play is not easily procurable. Here are two beautiful expressions, one of anticipated joy, one of the inexpressible secret of loveliness:

> "'Methought the Sun
> Arose this day with far more cheerful rays,
> With brighter beams, than usually it did;
> As if it would bring something of release
> Unto my cares; or else my spirit hath had
> Some manner of intelligence with Hope
> Wherewith my Heart is unacquainted yet.' (iii. 3.)

> "'Think not it was those colours, white and red,
> Laid but on flesh, that could affect me so,
> But something else, which thought holds under lock,
> And hath no key of words to open it.
> They are the smallest pieces of the mind
> That pass this narrow organ of the voice;
> The great remain behind in that vast orb
> Of th' apprehension, and are never born.' (iii. 5.)"

Coleridge[1] was at one with Wordsworth in praising Daniel's "natural language," and they do but echo the judgment of the poet's contemporaries, who spoke of him as "well-languaged," "choice in word," "in English very pure and

[1] "Read Daniel—the admirable Daniel—in his *Civil Wars* and *Triumphs of Hymen*. The style and language are just such as any very pure and manly writer of the present day—Wordsworth, for example—would use." And again, "His diction is pre-eminently pure" (Table Talk). See also the passage quoted in the notes to page 51.

Introduction

copious." And the praise is richly deserved. But it needs qualifying in two ways. The praise of Daniel's language must not be allowed to disguise the fact that the thought, which it clothes so fitly, is no less choice, or that there are frequent flashes of illuminating imagination.

> "And even now at this instant I confess,
> Palæmon, I do feel a certain touch
> Of comfort, which I fear to entertain,
> *Lest it should be some spy sent as a train*
> *To make discovery of what strength I am.*"
> (*H. T.*, iii. 4.)

> "And then to see how soon example will
> Disperse itself, being met with our desire;
> How soon it will enkindle others' ill,
> *Like naphtha that takes fire by sight of fire.*"
> (*Q. A.*, ii. 4.)

> "For Honour never brought Unworthiness
> Further than to the grave." (*Funeral Poem.*)

Of Daniel's tragedies and their relation to the contemporary drama it would be out of place to speak here, as the plays themselves are not in evidence; it must be sufficient to point in passing to the peculiar solemnity and weight given to the speeches by Daniel's practice of writing in quatrains (see p. 23). But a word may be said upon the lyrical choruses in *Cleopatra*, one of which is given at length on pp. 20-22. Most cultivated readers will feel their charm, though they will possibly find it difficult to explain where precisely the charm lies. Partly, no doubt, it may be due to the unusual and effective six-syllable metre, partly to the unusual and no less effective arrangement of rhymes, but beyond that there is little to which attention can be called unless it be the simple dignity of the thought and the simple dignity of the language in which it is clothed.

Entirely unlike the delicate finish of Daniel's work is the broad and free sweep of Drayton's mature style. It is no question with him of *nuances* whether of idea or expression. His Muse has no pallor of thought. His sentiments are those of the average healthy Englishman, and the form into which they are cast impresses by the vigour and raciness of the whole rather than by any peculiar felicity of individual parts. The spirit and movement of the *Ballad of Agincourt*, and, in less degree, of the *Virginia Voyage*, have long been recognised, and his love poems, though more loosely put together, have not a little of the rollicking ease that we associate with the Cavalier poets. This is one of Drayton's claims to recognition. Another is his fairy-poem, *Nymphidia*, which has many of the qualities necessary for success in so perilous a following of the great master — invention, grace, and humour. Finally, he deserves high praise for daring to turn his back on the Spenserian convention, and to write, in the *Muses' Elysium*, pastoral poems which, like those of Theocritus, deal with the lives and pursuits of simple country folk. Of the *Poly-Olbion* I would speak with respect, for it was admired by Charles Lamb. And I would admit that it is much easier reading than might be thought before attempting it. It has buoyancy and a fine flowing line, and the reader soon covers the ground. But the exercise is pretty much its own

Introduction

reward; there are few beauties on the road to justify one in taking that particular journey.

A word may be added as to the Editor's share in the following pages. Very great pains have been spent to make the text as accurate as possible. For the most part it has been transcribed from the best of the early copies; and as the spelling had to be modernised, and the punctuation adapted to the sense, the labour has not been light; and it can hardly be hoped that all inconsistency has been avoided. A reference to the notes will show that to several passages in Daniel the Editor has been fortunate in restoring the long-lost sense. The portrait of Daniel is from that by Cockson, prefixed to the 1609 edition of the *Civile Wars*. The woodcut of Drayton is from Hole's engraving in the Poems of 1613; the mezzotint is, by permission, from that prefixed to Dr Garnett's reprint of the *Battaile of Agincourt*.

YATTENDON RECTORY,
January 1899.

DANIEL.

1562. Samuel Daniel, born near Taunton, the son of John Daniel, a music-master.
1579. Goes as a commoner to Magdalen Hall, but leaves Oxford without a degree.
1585. Publishes a translation of *Imprese*, i.e. emblems, by Paulus Jovius, Bishop of Nocera.
1591. Twenty-seven of his sonnets printed at the end of Nash's edition of *Astrophel and Stella*.
1592. *Delia, contayning certaine sonnets* [50]. Dedicated to Mary, Countess of Pembroke, "Sidney's sister," at whose house at Wilton he was staying as tutor to William Herbert. The book was reprinted the same year with four additional sonnets, and *The Complaynt of Rosamond*.
1594. *Cleopatra*, added to an augmented reprint of *Delia* and *Rosamond*.
1595. *The Civile Wars between the two Houses of Lancaster and Yorke*; first four books, and then five.
1599. *Musophilus, or a General Defence of Learning. A Letter from Octavia to Marcus Antonius*.
1600. Becomes tutor to Lady Anne Clifford, daughter of the Countess of Cumberland.
1602. *The Defence of Ryme.*
1603. *A Panegyricke Congratulatorie. Poetical Epistles* (to Sir Thomas Egerton, Lord Henry Howard, the Countess of Cumberland, the Countess of Bedford, Lady Anne Clifford, the Earl of Southampton).
1604. Made censor of plays to the Queen's "children of the revels." *The Vision of the Twelve Goddesses*, a mask. *The Queens Arcadia*, a pastoral play.
1605. *The Tragedy of Philotas, Ulisses and the Syren*.
1607. Made one of the grooms of the Queen's privy chamber.
1609. Eight books of the *Civill Warres*.
1610. *Tethys Festival*, a mask.
1612-1617. *Collection of the Historie of England*, in prose.
1615. *Hymens Triumph*, a pastoral play.
1619. Oct., Daniel died at Beckington, where he had retired to farm.
1623. His brother published *The Whole Works of Samuel Daniel, Esquire, in poetrie*.

DRAYTON.

- 1563. Michael Drayton, born at Hartshill, near Atherstone, Warwickshire; of uncertain parentage; patronised in early boyhood by Sir Henry Goodere of Polesworth Hall, on the river Ancor, whose daughter Anne is certainly his "Idea." She married Sir Henry Rainsford.
- 1591. *The Harmonie of the Church*, paraphrases of Biblical songs. The edition was seized and burnt; why is not known. D. reprinted it in 1610.
- 1593. *Idea, the Shepherds Garland fashioned in nine Eglogs.* [The finest, containing the daffodil song, was added in 1606.] *Legend of Piers Gaveston.*
- 1594. *The Legend of Matilda. Ideas Mirrour: Amours in Quatorzains.* (53 Sonnets.)
- 1595. *Endimion and Phœbe, Ideas Latmus.*
- 1596. *Mortimeriados, The lamentable Civell Warres of Edward the Second and the Barrons*, written in rime-royal. *The Tragicall Legend of Robert, Duke of Normandy.*
- 1597. *Englands Heroicall Epistles.*
- 1600. *The History of Sir John Oldcastle*, a play in which D. collaborated.
- 1603. *To the Majestie of King James, a gratulatorie poem. The Barrons Wars in the Raigne of Edward the Second*, a re-written version of *Mortimeriados* in ottava rima.
- 1604. *The Owl.*
- 1606. *Poemes Lyrick and Pastorall; Odes and Eglogs.* Seven more odes were added in the collected volume of 1619.
- 1612. First eighteen songs of the *Poly-Olbion.*
- 1622. *Poly-Olbion* complete.
- 1627. A volume containing *The Battaile of Agincourt, The Miseries of Queene Margarete, Nimphidia, the Court of Fayrie, The Quest of Cynthia, The Shepheards Sirena, The Moonccalf,* and *Elegies.*
- 1630. *The Muses Elizium*, in ten "nimphalls," in a volume with *Noahs Floud, Moses his Birth and Miracles,* and *David and Goliah.*
- 1631. Dec. 23 [?], Drayton died.

A SELECTION FROM THE POEMS OF SAMUEL DANIEL

SONNETS TO DELIA

Unto the boundless ocean of thy beauty
    Runs this poor river, charged with streams of zeal,
    Returning thee the tribute of my duty,
    Which here my love, my youth, my plaints reveal.
Here I unclasp the book of my charged soul,
    Where I have cast th' accounts of all my care;
    Here have I summed my sighs; here I enroll
    How they were spent for thee; look what they are.
Look on the dear expences of my youth,
    And see how just I reckon with thine eyes;
    Examine well thy beauty with my truth,
    And cross my cares, ere greater sums arise.
Read it, sweet maid, though it be done but slightly;
Who can show all his love, doth love but lightly.

If so it hap this offspring of my care,
    These fatal anthems, lamentable songs,
    Come to their view who like afflicted are,
    Let them sigh for their own, and moan my wrongs.
But untouched hearts, with unaffected eye,
    Approach not to behold my heaviness:
    Clear-sighted you soon note what is awry,
    While blinded souls mine errors never guess.
You blinded souls whom Youth and Error lead!
    You out-cast Eaglets, dazzled with your sun!
    Do you, and none but you, my sorrows read;
    You best can judge the wrongs that she hath done.
That she hath done!—the motive of my pain:
Who, whilst I love, doth kill me with disdain.

These plaintive verse, the posts of my desire,
    Which haste for succour to her slow regard,
    Bear not report of any slender fire,
    Forging a grief to win a fame's reward.
Nor are my passions limned for outward hue,
    For that no colours can depaint my sorrows;
    DELIA herself, and all the world, may view
    Best in my face where cares have till'd deep furrows.
No bays I seek to deck my mourning brow,
    O clear-eyed Rector of the holy hill!
    My humble accents bear the olive bough
    Of intercession, but to move her will.
These lines I use to unburden mine own heart;
My love affects no fame, nor steams of art.

Whilst Youth and Error led my wandering mind,
    And set my thoughts in heedless ways to range,
    All unawares a goddess chaste I find,
    Diana-like, to work my sudden change.
For her no sooner had mine eyes bewrayed,
    But with disdain to see me in that place
    With fairest hand the sweet unkindest maid
    Cast water-cold disdain upon my face.
Which turned my sport into a heart's despair,
    Which still is chaced, while I have any breath,
    By mine own thoughts set on me by my fair:
    My thoughts, like hounds, pursue me to my death.
Those that I fostered of mine own accord
Are made by her to murder thus their lord.

Fair is my love, and cruel as she's fair;
    Her brow-shades frown, although her eyes are sunny;
    Her smiles are lightning though her pride despair;
    And her disdains are gall, her favours honey.
A modest maid, decked with a blush of honour,
    Whose feet do tread green paths of youth and love!
    The wonder of all eyes that look upon her;
    Sacred on earth, designed a saint above!
Chastity and Beauty, which were deadly foes,
    Live reconciled friends within her brow;
    And had she Pity to conjoin with those
    Then who had heard the plaints I utter now?
For had she not been fair, and thus unkind,
My Muse had slept, and none had known my mind.

If this be love, to draw a weary breath,
    Paint on floods till the shore cry to the air;
    With downward looks, still reading on the earth
    The sad memorials of my love's despair:
If this be love, to war against my soul,
    Lie down to wail, rise up to sigh and grieve,
    This never-resting stone of care to roll,
    Still to complain my griefs whilst none relieve.
If this be love to clothe me with dark thoughts,
    Haunting untrodden paths to wail apart;
    My pleasures horror, music tragic notes,
    Tears in mine eyes and sorrow at my heart.
If this be love, to live a living death:—
Then do I love and draw this weary breath.

My spotless love hovers with purest wings
    About the temple of the proudest frame,
    Where blaze those lights, fairest of earthly things,
    Which clear our clouded world with brightest flame.
My ambitious thoughts, confined in her face,
    Affect no honour but what she can give:
    My hopes do rest in limits of her grace;
    I weigh no comfort, unless she relieve.
For she, that can my heart imparadise,
    Holds in her fairest hand what dearest is;
    My fortune's-wheel's the circle of her eyes,
    Whose rolling grace deign once a turn of bliss!
All my life's sweet consists in her alone,
So much I love the most unloving one.

Behold what hap Pygmalion had to frame
    And carve his proper grief upon a stone!
    My heavy fortune is much like the same;
    I work on flint, and that's the cause I moan.
For hapless, lo! even with mine own desires
    I figured on the table of mine heart
    The fairest form that all the world admires;
    And so did perish by my proper art.
And still I toil, to change the marble breast
    Of her, whose sweetest grace I do adore;
    Yet cannot find her breathe unto my rest:
    Hard is her heart, and woe is me therefore!
But happy he that joyed his stone and art:
Unhappy I, to love a stony heart.

Why should I sing in verse, why should I frame
    These sad neglected notes for her dear sake?
    Why should I offer up unto her name
    The sweetest sacrifice my youth can make?
Why should I strive to make her live for ever
    That never deigns to give me joy to live?
    Why should my afflicted Muse so much endeavour
    Such honour unto cruelty to give?
If her defects have purchased her this fame
    What should her virtues do, her smiles, her love?
    If this her worst, how should her best inflame?
    What passions would her milder favours move?
Favours, I think, would sense quite overcome,
And that makes happy lovers ever dumb.

Since the first look that led me to this error,
    To this thoughts' maze, to my confusion tending,
    Still have I lived in grief, in hope, in terror,
    The circle of my sorrows never ending.
Yet cannot leave her love that holds me hateful ;
    Her eyes exact it, though her heart disdains me:
    See what reward he hath that serves the un-
        grateful !
    So true and loyal love no favour gains me.
Still must I whet my young desires abated
    Upon the flint of such a heart rebelling,
    And all in vain ; her pride is so innated,
    She yields no place at all for Pity's dwelling.
Oft have I told her that my soul did love her,
And that with tears, yet all this will not move her.

Restore thy tresses to the golden ore ;
    Yield Cytherea's son those arcs of love :
    Bequeath the heavens the stars that I adore ;
    And to the orient do thy pearls remove.
Yield thy hands' pride unto the ivory white ;
    To Arabian odours give thy breathing sweet ;
    Restore thy blush unto Aurora bright ;
    To Thetis give the honour of thy feet.
Let Venus have thy graces her resigned ;
    And thy sweet voice give back unto the spheres:
    But yet restore thy fierce and cruel mind
    To Hyrcan tigers and to ruthless bears.
Yield to the marble thy hard heart again ;
So shalt thou cease to plague and I to pain.

Time, cruel Time, come and subdue that brow,
    Which conquers all but thee ; and thee too stays
    As if she were exempt from Scythe or Bow,
    From Love or Years, unsubject to decays.
Or art thou grown in league with those fair eyes,
    That they may help thee to consume our days?
    Or dost thou spare her for her cruelties,
    Being merciless like thee, that no man weighs ?
And yet thou see'st thy power she disobeys ;
    Cares not for thee but lets thee waste in vain ;
    And prodigal of hours and years, betrays
    Beauty and Youth to Opinion and Disdain.
Yet spare her, Time ; let her exempted be ;
She may become more kind to thee or me.

Reign in my thoughts, fair hand, sweet eye, rare voice,
    Possess me whole, my heart's triumvirate :
    Yet heavy heart to make so hard a choice,
    Of such as spoil thy poor, afflicted state.
For whilst they strive which shall be lord of all,
    All my poor life by them is trodden down ;
    They all erect their trophies on my fall,
    And yield *me* nought, that gives them their renown.
When back I look I sigh my freedom past,
    And wail the state wherein I present stand,
    And see my fortune ever like to last,
    Finding me reined with such a heavy hand.
What can I do but yield ?—And yield I do,
And serve all three ; and yet they spoil me too.

Still in the trace of one perplexed thought,
    My ceaseless cares continually run on;
    Seeking in vain, what I have ever sought,
    One in my love and her hard heart still one.
I who did never joy in other sun,
    And have no stars but those that must fulfil
    The work of rigour, fatally begun
    Upon this heart, whom cruelty will kill.
Injurious DELIA, yet I love thee still;
    And will, whilst I shall draw this breath of mine:
    I'll tell the world, that I deserved but ill,
    And blame myself to excuse that heart of thine.
See then who sins the greater of us twain;
I in my love, or thou in thy disdain.

And yet I cannot reprehend the flight,
    Or blame the attempt presuming so to soar;
    The mounting venture for a high delight
    Did make the honour of the fall the more.
For who gets wealth that puts not from the shore?
    Danger hath honour, great designs their fame;
    Glory doth follow, courage goes before.
    And though the event oft answers not the same,
    Suffice that high attempts have never shame.
The mean observer, whom base safety keeps,
    Lives without honour, dies without a name,
    And in eternal darkness ever sleeps.
And therefore, DELIA, 'tis to me no blot
To have attempted though attained thee not.

Look, Delia, how we esteem the half-blown rose
    The image of thy blush, and summer's honour!
    Whilst yet her tender bud doth undisclose
    That full of beauty Time bestows upon her.
No sooner spreads her glory in the air
    But strait her wide-blown pomp comes to decline;
    She then is scorn'd that late adorned the fair;
    So fade the roses of those cheeks of thine.
No April can revive thy withered flowers
    Whose springing grace adorns thy glory now;
    Swift, speedy Time, feathered with flying hours,
    Dissolves the beauty of the fairest brow.
Then do not thou such treasure waste in vain,
But love now, whilst thou mayst be loved again.

But love whilst that thou mayst be lov'd again,
    Now whilst thy May hath filled thy lap with flowers;
    Now whilst thy beauty bears without a stain
    Now use the summer smiles ere winter lowers.
And whilst thou spread'st unto the rising sun
    The fairest flower that ever saw the light,
    Now joy thy time before thy sweet be done;
    And, Delia, think thy morning must have night,
And that thy brightness sets at length to west
    When thou wilt close up that which now thou show'st,
    And think the same becomes thy fading best,
    Which then shall most enveil and shadow most.
Men do not weigh the stalk for that it was,
When once they find her flower, her glory, pass.

When men shall find thy flower, thy glory, pass,
    And thou with careful brow sitting alone
    Received hast this message from thy glass
    That tells the truth and says that all is gone;
Fresh shalt thou see in me the wounds thou mad'st,
    Though spent thy flame, in me the heat remain-
        ing;
    I that have loved thee thus before thou fad'st
    My faith shall wax, when thou art in thy waning.
The world shall find this miracle in me,
    That fire can burn when all the matter's spent:
    Then what my faith hath been thy self shalt see,
    And that thou wast unkind thou mayst repent.
Thou mayst repent that thou hast scorned my tears
When winter snows upon thy sable hairs.

When winter snows upon thy sable hairs,
    And frost of age hath nipt thy beauties near;
    When dark shall seem thy day that never clears,
    And all lies withered that was held so dear;
Then take this picture which I here present thee
    Limnèd with a pencil not all unworthy;
    Here see the gifts that God and Nature lent thee;
    Here read thyself and what I suffered for thee.
This may remain thy lasting monument,
    Which happily posterity may cherish;
    These colours with thy fading are not spent;
    These may remain when thou and I shall perish
If they remain, then thou shalt live thereby;
They will remain, and so thou canst not die.

Care-charmer Sleep, son of the sable Night,
    Brother to Death, in silent darkness born:
    Relieve my languish, and restore the light;
    With dark forgetting of my care, return!
And let the day be time enough to mourn
    The shipwreck of my ill-adventured youth:
    Let waking eyes suffice to wail their scorn,
    Without the torment of the night's untruth.
Cease, dreams, the images of day-desires,
    To model forth the passions of the morrow;
    Never let rising sun approve you liars,
    To add more grief to aggravate my sorrow.
Still let me sleep, embracing clouds in vain;
And never wake to feel the day's disdain.

Most fair and lovely maid, look from the shore,
    See thy Leander striving in these waves!
    Poor soul quite spent whose force can do no more!
    Now send forth hope, for now calm pity saves.
And waft him to thee with those lovely eyes,
    A happy convoy to a holy land:
    Now show thy power, and where thy virtue lies;
    To save thine own, stretch out the fairest hand.
Stretch out the fairest hand, a pledge of peace,
    That hand that darts so right and never misses.
    I shall forget old wrongs, my griefs shall cease,
    And that which gave me wounds, I'll give it kisses.
Once let the Ocean of my cares find shore,
That thou be pleased, and I may sigh no more.

Read in my face a volume of despairs,
    The wailing Iliads of my tragic woe,
    Drawn with my blood and painted with my cares,
    Wrought by her hand that I have honoured so.
Who whilst I burn, she sings at my soul's wrack,
    Looking aloft from turret of her pride;
    There my soul's tyrant joys her in the sack
    Of her own seat, whereof I made her guide.
There do these smokes that from affliction rise
    Serve as an incense to a cruel dame,
    A sacrifice thrice grateful to her eyes,
    Because their power serve to exact the same.
Thus ruins she, to satisfy her will,
The temple where her name was honoured still.

I must not grieve my Love, whose eyes would read
    Lines of delight, whereon her youth might smile;
    Flowers have a time before they come to seed
    And she is young, and now must sport the while.
And sport, sweet maid, in season of these years
    And learn to gather flowers before they wither;
    And where the sweetest blossom first appears
    Let Love and Youth conduct thy pleasures thither.
Lighten forth smiles to clear the clouded air
    And calm the tempest which my sighs do raise:
    Pity and smiles do best become the fair;
    Pity and smiles must only yield thee praise.
Make me to say, when all my griefs are gone,
Happy the heart that sighed for such a one.

Beauty, sweet love, is like the morning dew,
   Whose short refresh upon the tender green
   Cheers for a time, but till the sun doth shew,
   And straight 'tis gone as it had never been.
Soon doth it fade that makes the fairest flourish;
   Short is the glory of the blushing rose:
   The hue which thou so carefully dost nourish,
   Yet which at length thou must be forced to lose.
When thou, surcharged with burden of thy years,
   Shalt bend thy wrinkles homeward to the earth,
   And that in beauty's lease expired appears
   The date of age, the calends of our death;—
But ah! no more; this must not be foretold:
For women grieve to think they must be old.

At the Author's Going into Italy

And whither, poor forsaken, wilt thou go,
   To go from sorrow and thine own distress,
   When every place presents like face of woe
   And no remove can make thy sorrows less?
Yet go, forsaken; leave these woods, these plains,
   Leave her and all, and all for her, that leaves
   Thee and thy love forlorn, and both disdains;
   And of both wrongful deems and ill conceives.
Seek out some place; and see if any place
   Can give the least release unto thy grief,
   Convey thee from the thought of thy disgrace,
   Steal from thyself, and be thy care's own thief.
But yet what comforts shall I hereby gain?
Bearing the wound, I needs must feel the pain.

At the Author's Being in Italy.

Drawn with the attractive virtue of her eyes,
    My touched heart turns it to that happy coast—
    My joyful North, where all my fortune lies,
    The level of my hopes desired most:
There where my DELIA fairer than the sun,
    Decked with her youth whereon the world doth smile,
    Joys in that honour which her eyes have won,
    The eternal wonder of our happy isle!
Flourish, fair Albion, glory of the North!
    Neptune's best darling, held between his arms:
    Divided from the world as better worth;
    Kept for himself, defended from all harms.
Still let disarmed Peace deck her and thee;
And Muse-foe Mars abroad far fostered be.

Let others sing of Knights and Paladins
    In aged accents and untimely words;
    Paint shadows in imaginary lines
    Which well the reach of their high wits records:
But I must sing of thee, and those fair eyes
    Authentic shall my verse in time to come;
    When yet th' unborn shall say, Lo where she lies,
    Whose beauty made him speak that else was dumb.
These are the arcs, the trophies I erect,
    That fortify thy name against old age;
    And these thy sacred virtues must protect
    Against the dark, and Time's consuming rage.
Though the error of my youth in them appear,
Suffice they shew I lived and loved thee dear.

As to the Roman that would free his land
   His error was his honour and renown,
   And more the fame of his mistaking hand
   Than if he had the tyrant overthrown;
So, DELIA, hath mine error made me known,
   And my deceived attempt deserved more fame
   Than if I had the victory mine own,
   And thy hard heart had yielded up the same.
And so likewise renowned is thy blame;
   Thy cruelty, thy glory. O strange case,
   That errors should be graced, that merit shame,
   And sin of frowns bring honour to the face!
Yet happy, DELIA, that thou wast unkind,
Though happier far, if thou wouldst change thy mind.

From THE COMPLAINT OF ROSAMOND

Rosamond Complains

I would to God my foot had never moved
From country-safety, from the fields of rest;
To know the danger to be highly loved,
And live in pomp to brave among the best;
Happy for me, better had I been blest,
   If I unluckily had never strayed,
   But lived at home a happy country-maid;

Whose unaffected innocency thinks
No guileful fraud as doth the courtly liver;
She's decked with truth; the river where she
    drinks
Doth serve her for her glass, her counsel-giver;
She loves sincerely and is lovéd ever.
   Her days are peace, and so she ends her breath,—
   True life that knows not what's to die till death.

King Henry meets the Bier

Amazed he stands, nor voice nor body stirs;
Words had no passage, tears no issue found;
For sorrow shut up words, wrath kept in tears;
Confused affects each other do confound;
Opprest with grief, his passions had no bound.
   Striving to tell his woes, words would not come;
   For light cares speak when mighty griefs are
     dumb.

At length extremity breaks out a way
Through which th' imprisoned voice, with tears
  attended,
Wails out a sound that sorrows do bewray;
With arms across, and eyes to heaven bended,
Vapouring out sighs that to the skies ascended;
  Sighs (the poor ease calamity affords)
  Which serve for speech when sorrow wanteth
    words.

"O heavens," quoth he, "why do mine eyes behold
The hateful rays of this unhappy sun?
Why have I light to see my sins controlled
With blood of mine own shame thus vildly done!
How can my sight endure to look thereon?
  Why doth not black eternal darkness hide
  That from mine eyes my heart cannot abide?

"What saw my life wherein my soul might joy?
What had my days, whom troubles still afflicted,
But only this, to counterpoise annoy?
This joy, this hope, which Death hath interdicted;
This sweet, whose loss hath all distress inflicted;
  This, that did season all my sour of life,
  Vexed still at home with broils, abroad in strife?

"Vexed still at home with broils, abroad in strife,
Dissension in my blood, jars in my bed;
Distrust at board, suspecting still my life,
Spending the night in horror, days in dread,
Such life hath Tyrants and this life I led;
  These miseries go masked in glittering shows,
  Which wise men see, the vulgar little knows."

Thus, as these passions do him overwhelm,
He draws him near the body to behold it:
And as the vine married unto the elm
With strict embraces, so doth he enfold it;
And as he in his careful arms doth hold it,
    Viewing the face that even Death commends,
    On senseless lips millions of kisses spends.

"Pitiful mouth," saith he, "that living gavest
The sweetest comfort that my soul could wish;
O be it lawful now that dead thou havest
This sorrowing farewell of a dying kiss.
And you fair eyes, containers of my bliss,
    Motives of love, born to be matched never,
    Entombed in your sweet circles sleep for ever.

"Ah, how methinks I see Death dallying seeks
To entertain itself in Love's sweet place;
Decayed roses of discoloured cheeks
Do yet retain dear notes of former grace;
And ugly death sits fair within her face;
    Sweet remnants resting of vermilion red,
    That Death itself doubts whether she be dead.

"Wonder of beauty, oh, receive these plaints,
These obsequies, the last that I shall make thee;
For lo, my soul that now already faints
(That loved thee living, dead will not forsake thee)
Hastens her speedy course to overtake thee.
    I'll meet my death, and free myself thereby;
    For, ah, what can he do that cannot die?

"Yet ere I die thus much my soul doth vow,
Revenge shall sweeten death with ease of mind;
And I will cause posterity shall know
How fair thou wert above all women-kind;
And after ages monuments shall find
   Shewing thy beauty's title (not thy name)
   Rose of the world that sweetened so the same."

From THE TRAGEDY OF CLEOPATRA

Chorus

Then thus we have beheld
Th' accomplishment of woes,
The full of ruin and
The worst of worst of ills:
And seen all hope expelled,
That ever sweet repose
Shall repossess the land
That Desolation fills;
And where Ambition spills
With uncontrolled hand
All th' issue of all those
That so long rule have held:
To make us no more us,
But clean confound us thus.

And can'st, O Nilus, thou
Father of floods, endure
That yellow Tiber should
With sandy streams rule thee?
Wilt thou be pleased to bow
To him those feet so pure,
Whose unknown head we hold
A power divine to be?

Thou that did'st ever see
Thy free banks uncontrolled,
Live under thine own cure;
Ah, wilt thou bear it now?
And now wilt yield thy streams
A prey to other reams?[1]

Draw back thy waters' flow
To thy concealed head;
Rocks strangle up thy waves,
Stop cataracts thy fall,
And turn thy courses so
That sandy deserts dead
(The world of dust that craves
To swallow thee up all)
May drink so much as shall
Revive from vasty graves
A living green, which spread
Far flourishing may grow
On that wide face of death,
Where nothing now draws breath.

Fatten some people there,
Even as thou us hast done,
With plenty's wanton store,
And feeble luxury;
And them as us prepare
Fit for the day of moan,
Respected not before.
Leave levelled Egypt dry,
A barren prey to lie,
Wasted for evermore;

[1] *i.e.* realms.

Of plenties yielding none
To recompense the care
Of victor's greedy lust,
And bring forth nought but dust.

   And so, O leave to be,
Sith thou art what thou art;
Let not our race possess
The inheritance of shame,
The fee of sin, that we
Have left them for their part.
The yoke of whose distress
Must still upbraid our blame,
Telling from whom it came.
Our weight of wantonness
Lies heavy on their heart,
Who nevermore shall see
The glory of that worth
They left, who brought us forth.

   O then, all-seeing light,
High President of heaven,
You Magistrates, the stars,
Of that eternal court
Of Providence and Right,—
Are these the bounds ye have given
Th' untranspassable bars
That limit pride so short?
Is greatness of this sort,
That greatness greatness mars,
And wracks itself, self-driven
On rocks of her own might?
Doth Order order so
Disorder's overthrow?

The Death of Cleopatra

Well, in I went, where brighter than the sun
Glittering in all her pompous rich array
Great Cleopatra sat, as if she had won
Cæsar, and all the world beside, this day:
Even as she was when on thy crystal streams,
Clear Cydnus, she did shew what earth could shew,
When Asia all amazed in wonder deems
Venus from heaven was come on earth below.
Even as she went at first to meet her love,
So goes she now [at last] again to find him;
But that first did her greatness only prove,
This last her love that could not live behind him.
Yet as she sat, the doubt of my good speed
Detracts much from the sweetness of her look;
Cheer-marrer Care did then such passions breed
That made her eye bewray the grief she took.
But she no sooner sees me in the place,
But straight her sorrow-clouded brow she clears,
Lightening a smile from out a stormy face,
Which all her tempest-beaten senses cheers.
    Look how a strayed perplexéd traveller
When chased by thieves, and even at point of taking,
Descrying suddenly some town not far,
Or some unlooked-for aid to him-ward making;
Cheers up his tired spirits, thrusts forth his strength,
To meet that good that comes in so good hour:
Such was her joy, perceiving now at length
Her honour was to escape so proud a power.
Forth from her seat she hastes to meet the present
And as one over-joyed she caught it straight

And with a smiling cheer in action pleasant
Looking among the figs, finds the deceit.
And seeing there the ugly, venomous beast,
Nothing dismayed, she stays and views it well;
At length the extremest of her passion ceased
When she began with words her joy to tell:
  "O rarest beast," saith she, "that Afric breeds
How dearly welcome art thou unto me!
The fairest creature that fair Nilus feeds
Methinks I see, in now beholding thee.
What though the ever-erring world doth deem
That angered Nature framed thee but in spite,
Little they know what they so light esteem,
That never learned the wonder of thy might.
Better than Death Death's office thou dischargest,
That with one gentle touch canst free our breath,
And in a pleasing sleep our soul enlargest,
Making ourselves not privy to our death.
If Nature erred, O then how happy error!
Thinking to make thee worst, she made thee best;
Sith thou best free'st us from our live's worst terror,
In sweetly bringing souls to quiet rest.
Therefore come thou, of wonders wonder chief,
That open canst with such an easy key
The door of life,—come, gentle cunning thief,
That from ourselves so steal'st ourselves away."
  With that she bares her arm, and offer makes
To touch her death, yet at the touch withdraws,
And, seeming more to speak, occasion takes,
Willing to die, and willing too to pause.
  Look how a mother at her son's departing,
For some far voyage bent to get him fame,
Doth entertain him with an idle parling,
And still doth speak, and still speaks but the same;

Now bids farewell, and now recalls him back,
Tells what was told, and bids again farewell,
And yet again recalls; for still doth lack
Something that Love would fain, and cannot, tell.
Pleased he should go, yet cannot let him go.—
So she, although she knew there was no way
But this, yet this she could not handle so
But she must shew that life desired delay.
Fain would she entertain the time as now,
And now would fain that Death should seize upon
    her
Whilst I might see presented in her brow
The doubtful combat tried 'twixt Life and Honour.
[Till] sharply blaming of her rebel powers,
    "False Flesh," saith she, "and what! dost
      thou conspire
With Cæsar too, as thou wert none of ours,
To work my shame, and hinder my desire?
Wilt thou retain in closure of thy veins
That enemy base Life, to let my good?
No, know there is a greater power constrains
Than can be counter-checked with fearful blood.
For to the mind that's great nothing seems great:
And seeing death to be the last of woes,
And life lasting disgrace, which I shall get,
What do I lose that have but life to lose!"
    This having said, strengthened in her own heart
And union of herself, senses in one
Charging together, she performs that part
That hath so great a part of glory won;
And so receives the deadly poisoning touch,
That touch that tried the gold of her love pure;
And hath confirmed her honour to be such
As must a wonder to all worlds endure.

Chorus

The scene is broken down
And all uncovered lies;
The purple actors known
Scarce men, whom men despise.
   The complots of the wise
Prove imperfection's smoke:
And all what wonder gave
To pleasure-gazing eyes
Lies scattered, dashed, all broke.
Thus much beguiled have
Poor unconsiderate wights
These momentary pleasures, fugitive delights.

From THE CIVIL WARS
King Richard II. led to London

Straight towards London, in this heat of pride,
They forward set, as they had fore-decreed;
With whom the captive King, constrain'd, must ride,
Most meanly mounted on a simple steed:
Degraded of all grace and ease beside,
Thereby neglect of all respect to breed.
For th' over-spreading pomp of prouder might
Must darken weakness, and debase his sight.

Approaching near the city he was met-
With all the sumptuous shews joy could devise;
Where new desire to please did not forget
To pass the usual pomp of former guise.
Striving applause, as out of prison let,
Runs on, beyond all bounds, to novelties;
And voice, and hands, and knees, and all do now
A strange deformed form of welcome show.

And manifold confusion running greets,
Shouts, cries, claps hands, thrusts, strives, and presses near:
Houses impov'rish'd were to enrich the streets,
And streets left naked, that (unhappy) were
Plac'd from the sight where joy with wonder meets;
Where all of all degrees strive to appear;
Where divers-speaking zeal one murmur finds,
In undistinguish'd voice to tell their minds.

He that in glory of his fortune sat,
Admiring what he thought could never be,
Did feel his blood within salute his state,
And lift up his rejoicing soul, to see
So many hands and hearts congratulate
Th' advancement of his long-desir'd degree;
When, prodigal of thanks, in passing by,
He re-salutes them all with cheerful eye.

Behind him, all aloof, came pensive on
The unregarded King; that drooping went
Alone, and (but for spite) scarce look'd upon:
Judge, if he did more envy, or lament!
See what a wondrous work this day is done!
Which th' image of both fortunes doth present:
In th' one to shew the best of glory's face,
In th' other worse than worst of all disgrace.

His Foreboding of Death

Whether the soul receives intelligence
By her near genius, of the body's end,
And so imparts a sadness to the sense,
Fore-going ruin, whereto it doth tend:
Or whether nature else hath conference
With profound sleep, and so doth warning send
By prophetizing dreams, what hurt is near,
And gives the heavy careful heart to fear;

However, so it is the now sad King
(Toss'd here and there, his quiet to confound)
Feels a strange weight of sorrows gathering
Upon his trembling heart, and sees no ground;

Feels sudden terror bring cold shivering:
Lists not to eat; still muses; sleeps unsound:
His senses droop, his steady eyes unquick;
And much he ails, and yet he is not sick.

The morning of that day which was his last,
After a weary rest rising to pain,
Out at a little grate his eyes he cast
Upon those bord'ring hills, and open plain,
And views the town, and sees how people pass'd;
Where others' liberty makes him complain
The more his own, and grieves his soul the more;
Conferring captive crowns with freedom poor.

"O happy man," saith he, "that lo I see
Grazing his cattle in those pleasant fields!
If he but knew his good, how blessed he,
That feels not what affliction greatness yields!
Other than what he is he would not be,
Nor change his state with him that sceptres wields.
Thine, thine, is that true life . . . That is to live
To rest secure, and not rise up to grieve.

"Thou sitt'st at home safe by thy quiet fire,
And hear'st of others' harms, but feelest none;
And there thou tell'st of kings, and who aspire,
Who fall, who rise, who triumphs, who do moan.
Perhaps thou talk'st of me, and dost enquire
Of my restraint; why here I live alone;
And pitiest this my miserable fall:
For pity must have part; envy not all.

"Thrice happy you, that look as from the shore,
And have no venture in the wreck you see;
No interest, no occasion to deplore
Other men's travels, while yourselves sit free.

How much doth your sweet rest make us the more
To see our misery, and what we be!
Whose blinded greatness ever in turmoil,
Still seeking happy life, makes life a toil."

The Death of Talbot

To whom th' aggrieved son (as if disgrac'd)—
"Ah! Father, have you then selected me
To be the man, whom you would have displac'd
Out of the roll of immortality?
What have I done this day, that hath defac'd
My worth; that my hands' work despis'd should be?
God shield I should bear home a coward's name:
He long enough hath liv'd, who dies with fame."

At which the father, touch'd with sorrowing joy,
Turn'd him about (shaking his head) and says,
"O my dear son, worthy a better day,
To enter thy first youth in hard assays!"
And now hath wrath, impatient of delay,
Begun the fight, and farther speeches stays.
Fury thrusts on; striving whose sword should be
First warmed in the wounds of th' enemy.

Hotly these small (but mighty-minded) bands
(As if ambitious now of death) do strain
Against innumerable armed hands,
And gloriously a wondrous fight maintain;
Rushing on all whatever strength withstands,
Whetting their wrath on blood, and on disdain;
And so far thrust, that hard 'twere to descry,
Whether they more desire to kill, or die.

Frank of their own, greedy of others' blood,
No stroke they give but wounds, no wound but kills:
Near to their hate, close to their work they stood;
Hit where they would, their hand obeys their wills;
Scorning the blow from far that doth no good,
Loathing the crack, unless some blood it spills:
No wounds could let out life that wrath held in,
Till others' wounds reveng'd did first begin.

So much true resolution wrought in those
Who had made covenant with death before,
That their small number (scorning so great foes)
Made France most happy, that there were no more;
And fortune doubt to whom she might dispose
That weary day; or unto whom restore
The glory of a conquest dearly bought,
Which scarce the conqueror could think well got.

For as with equal rage, and equal might,
Two adverse winds combat, with billows proud,
And neither yield: seas, skies maintain like fight,
Wave against wave oppos'd, and cloud to cloud:
So war both sides with obstinate despite,
With like revenge; and neither party bow'd:
Fronting each other with confounding blows,
No wound one sword unto the other owes.

Whilst Talbot (whose fresh ardour having got
A marvellous advantage of his years)
Carries his unfelt age as if forgot,
Whirling about where any need appears.
His hand, his eye, his wits all present, wrought
The function of the glorious part he bears:
Now urging here, now cheering there, he flies;
Unlocks the thickest troops, where most force lies.

In midst of wrath, of wounds, of blood and death
There is he most, where as he may do best;
And there the closest ranks he severeth,
Drives back the stoutest pow'rs that forward press'd:
There makes his sword his way—there laboureth
Th' infatigable hand that never ceas'd;
Scorning unto his mortal wounds to yield,
Till death became best master of the field.

Then like a sturdy oak, that having long
Against the wars of fiercest winds made head,
When with some forc'd tempestuous rage more strong
His down-borne top comes over-mastered,
All the near bord'ring trees, he stood among,
Crush'd with his weighty fall, lie ruined:
So lay his spoils, all round about him slain
To adorn his death, that could not die in vain.

EPISTLE TO THE LADY MARGARET, COUNTESS OF CUMBERLAND

He that of such a height hath built his mind,
And rear'd the dwelling of his thoughts so strong,
As neither fear nor hope can shake the frame
Of his resolved pow'rs; nor all the wind
Of vanity or malice pierce to wrong
His settled peace, or to disturb the same:
What a fair seat hath he, from whence he may
The boundless wastes and wilds of man survey?
    And with how free an eye doth he look down
Upon these lower regions of turmoil?
Where all the storms of passions mainly beat
On flesh and blood: where honour, pow'r, renown
Are only gay afflictions, golden toil;
Where greatness stands upon as feeble feet
As frailty doth; and only great doth seem
To little minds, who do it so esteem.
    He looks upon the mightiest monarchs' wars
But only as on stately robberies;
Where evermore the fortune that prevails
Must be the right: the ill-succeeding mars
The fairest and the best-fac'd enterprize.
Great pirate Pompey lesser pirates quails:

Epistle to Countess of Cumberland

Justice, he sees (as if seduced), still
Conspires with pow'r, whose cause must not be ill.
    He sees the face of Right t' appear as manifold
As are the passions of uncertain man;
Who puts it in all colours, all attires,
To serve his ends, and make his courses hold.
He sees, that let deceit work what it can,
Plot and contrive base ways to high desires,
That the all-guiding Providence doth yet
All disappoint, and mocks this smoke of wit.
    Nor is he mov'd with all the thunder-cracks
Of tyrants' threats, or with the surly brow
Of pow'r, that proudly sits on others' crimes;
Charg'd with more crying sins than those he checks.
The storms of sad confusion, that may grow
Up in the present for the coming times,
Appal not him; that hath no side at all,
But of himself, and knows the worst can fall.
    Altho' his heart, so near allied to earth,
Cannot but pity the perplexed state
Of troublous and distress'd mortality,
That thus make way unto the ugly birth
Of their own sorrows, and do still beget
Affliction upon imbecility:
Yet seeing thus the course of things must run,
He looks thereon not strange, but as fore-done.
    And whilst distraught ambition compasses,
And is encompass'd; whilst as craft deceives,
And is deceiv'd; whilst man doth ransack man,
And builds on blood, and rises by distress;
And th' inheritance of desolation leaves
To great-expecting hopes: he looks thereon,
As from the shore of peace, with unwet eye,
And bears no venture in impiety.

Epistle to Countess of Cumberland

    Thus, Madam, fares the man that hath prepar'd
A rest for his desires; and sees all things
Beneath him; and hath learn'd this book of man,
Full of the notes of frailty; and compar'd
The best of glory with her sufferings:
By whom, I see, you labour all you can
To plant your heart; and set your thoughts as near
His glorious mansion, as your pow'rs can bear.

    Which, Madam, are so soundly fashioned
By that clear judgment, that hath carried you
Beyond the feeble limits of your kind,
As they can stand against the strongest head
Passion can make; inur'd to any hue
The world can cast; that cannot cast that mind
Out of her form of goodness, that doth see
Both what the best and worst of earth can be.

    Which makes, that whatsoever here befals,
You in the region of yourself remain:
Where no vain breath of th' impudent molests,
That hath secur'd within the brazen walls
Of a clear conscience, that without all stain
Rises in peace, in innocency rests;
Whilst all what malice from without procures,
Shews her own ugly heart, but hurts not yours.

    And whereas none rejoice more in revenge
Than women use to do; yet you well know,
That wrong is better check'd by being contemn'd,
Than being pursu'd; leaving to him to avenge,
To whom it appertains. Wherein you show,
How worthily your clearness hath condemn'd
Base malediction, living in the dark,
That at the rays of goodness still doth bark.

    Knowing the heart of man is set to be
The centre of his world, about the which

36 Epistle to Countess of Cumberland

These revolutions of disturbances
Still roll; where all th' aspects of misery
Predominate; whose strong effects are such,
As he must bear, being powerless to redress:
And that unless above himself he can
Erect himself, how poor a thing is man!
    And how turmoil'd they are that level lie
With earth, and cannot lift themselves from thence;
That never are at peace with their desires,
But work beyond their years; and ev'n deny
Dotage her rest, and hardly will dispense
With death. That when ability expires,
Desire lives still—so much delight they have,
To carry toil and travail to the grave.
    Whose ends you see; and what can be the best
They reach unto, when they have cast the sum
And reck'nings of their glory. And you know,
This floating life hath but this port of rest,
A heart prepar'd, that fears no ill to come.
And that man's greatness rests but in his show,
The best of all whose days consumed are,
Either in war, or peace conceiving war.
    This concord, Madam, of a well-tun'd mind
Hath been so set by that all-working hand
Of heav'n, that tho' the world hath done his worst
To put it out by discords most unkind;
Yet doth it still in perfect union stand
With God and man; nor ever will be forc'd
From that most sweet accord; but still agree,
Equal in fortune's inequality.
    And this note, Madam, of your worthiness
Remains recorded in so many hearts,
As time nor malice cannot wrong your right,

Epistle to Countess of Cumberland

In th' inheritance of fame you must possess :
You that have built you by your great deserts,
Out of small means, a far more exquisite
And glorious dwelling for your honour'd name,
Than all the gold of leaden minds can frame.

From MUSOPHILUS

Non omnis moriar

Short-breathed Mortality would yet extend
That span of life so far forth as it may;
And rob her fate, seek to beguile her end
Of some few lingering days of after-stay;
That all this Little-all might not descend
Into the dark an universal prey:
And give our labours yet this poor delight
That when our days do end, they are not done;
And though we die, we shall not perish quite,
But live two lives where others have but one.

Literature

O blessed Letters, that combine in one
All ages past, and make one live with all!
By you we do confer with who are gone,
And the dead-living unto council call:
By you the unborn shall have communion
Of what we feel and what doth us befall.

Soul of the World, Knowledge, without thee
What hath the earth that truly glorious is?
Why should our pride make such a stir to be,
To be forgot? What good is like to this,
To do worthy the writing, and to write
Worthy the reading, and the world's delight!

Religion

    Sacred Religion! Mother of Form and Fear!
How gorgeously sometimes dost thou sit decked!
What pompous vestures do we make thee wear,
What stately piles we prodigal erect,
How sweet perfumed thou art, how shining clear,
How solemnly observed, with what respect!
    Another time all plain, all quite thread-bare;
Thou must have all within, and nought without;
Sit poorly without light, disrobed,—no care
Of outward grace, to amuse the poor devout;
Powerless, unfollowed; scarcely men can spare
The necessary rites to set thee out!

φωνᾶντα συνετοῖσι

    And for the few that only lend their ear,
That few is all the world; which with a few
Do ever live, and move, and work, and stir.
    This is the heart doth feel, and only know
The rest of all that only bodies bear,
Roll up and down, and fill but up the row;
    And serves as others' members, not their own,
The instruments of those that do direct.
Then what disgrace is this, not to be known
To those know not to give themselves respect?
And though they swell with pomp of folly blown,
They live ungraced, and die but in neglect.
    And for my part, if only one allow
The care my labouring spirits take in this;
He is to me a theatre large enow,
And his applause only sufficient is;
All my respect is bent but to his brow;
That is my all, and all I am is his.

English Poetry

Power above Powers! O heavenly Eloquence!
That with the strong rein of commanding words
Dost manage, guide, and master the eminence
Of men's affections, more than all their swords!
Shall we not offer to thy excellence
The richest treasure that our wit affords?

Thou that can'st do much more with one poor pen,
Than all the powers of Princes can effect,
And draw, divert, dispose, and fashion men,
Better than force or rigour can direct!
Should we this ornament of glory, then,
As the unmaterial fruits of shades, neglect?

Or should we careless come behind the rest
In power of words, that go before in worth;
Whenas our accent's equal to the best,
Is able greater wonders to bring forth?
When all that ever hotter spirits exprest
Comes bettered by the patience of the North.

From THE EPISTLE TO SIR THOMAS EGERTON

LAW

Now when we see the most combining band,
The strongest fastening of Society,
Law, whereon all this frame of men doth stand,
Remain concussed with uncertainty;
And seem to foster, rather than withstand,
Contention, and embrace obscurity,
Only to afflict, and not to fashion us,
Making her cure far worse than the disease:

As if she had made covenant with wrong
To part the prey made on our weaknesses;
And suffered falsehood to be armed as strong
Unto the combat as is righteousness;
Or suited her, as if she did belong
Unto our passions, and did even profess
Contention, as her only mystery,
Which she restrains not, but doth multiply;—

Was she the same she is now in ages past,
Or was she less when she was used less?
And grows as malice grows, and so comes cast
Just to the form of our unquietness?
Or made more slow the more that strife runs fast,
Staying to undo us ere she will redress?

That the ill she checks seems suffered to be ill,
When it yields greater gain than goodness will.

Must there be still some discord mixt among
The harmony of men whose mood accords
Best with contention, tuned to a note of wrong,
That when war fails, peace must make war with
     words,
And be armed unto destruction even as strong
As were in ages past our civil swords ;
Making as deep although unbleeding wounds
That whenas fury fails, wisdom confounds.

If it be wisdom and not cunning this
Which so embroils the state of Truth with brawls,
And wraps it up in strange confusedness
As if it lived immured within the walls
Of hideous terms, framed out of barbarousness
And foreign customs, the memorials
Of our subjection, and could never be
Delivered but by wrangling subtilty.

Whereas it dwells free in the open plain
Uncurious, gentle, easy of access :
Certain unto itself ; of equal vein ;
One face, one colour, one assuredness.
It's falsehood that is intricate and vain,
And needs these labyrinths of subtleness :
For where the cunning'st coverings most appear,
It argues still that all is not sincere.

Epistle to Sir Thomas Egerton

JUSTICE

All glory else besides ends with our breath,
And men's respects scarce brings us to our grave:
But this of doing good must outlive death
And have a right out of the right it gave.
Though th' act but few, th' example profiteth
Thousands that shall thereby a blessing have.
The world's respect grows not but on deserts;
Power may have knees, but Justice hath our hearts.

From THE TRAGEDY OF PHILOTAS
Chorus

How dost thou wear and weary out thy days,
Restless ambition, never at an end!
Whose travels no Herculean pillar stays,
But still beyond thy rest thy labours tend;
Above good fortune thou thy hopes dost raise,
Still climbing, and yet never canst ascend:
    For when thou hast attained unto the top
    Of thy desires, thou hast not yet got up.

That height of fortune either is controlled
By some more powerful overlooking eye,
That doth the fulness of thy grace withhold,
Or counter-checked with some concurrency;
That it doth cost far more ado to hold
The height attained, than was to get so high;
    Where stand thou canst not but with careful toil,
    Nor loose thy hold without thy utter spoil.

There dost thou struggle with thine own distrust
And others' jealousies; there counterplot
Against some underworking pride, that must
Supplanted be, or else thou standest not;
There wrong is played with wrong, and he that thrust
Down others comes himself to have that lot.
    The same concussion doth afflict his breast
    That others shook; oppression is oppressed.

The Tragedy of Philotas

That either Happiness dwells not so high,
Or else above, whereto Pride cannot rise:
And that the highest of man's felicity
But in the region of Affliction lies:
And that we climb but up to misery.
High fortunes are but high calamities!
    It is not in that sphere where Peace doth move;
    Rest dwells below it, Happiness above.

ULYSSES AND THE SIREN

SIREN

Come, worthy Greek! Ulysses, come;
Possess these shores with me!
The winds and seas are troublesome
And here we may be free!
    Here may we sit and view their toil
That travail on the deep,
And joy the day in mirth the while
And spend the night in sleep.

ULYSSES

Fair nymph, if fame or honour were
To be attained with ease,
Then would I come and rest [me there]
And leave such toils as these.
    But here it dwells, and here must I
With danger seek it forth:
To spend the time luxuriously
Becomes not men of worth.

SIREN

Ulysses, O be not deceived
With that unreal name;
This honour is a thing conceived
And rests on others' fame;

Ulysses and the Siren

Begotten only to molest
Our peace, and to beguile
The best thing of our life—our rest,
And give us up to toil.

ULYSSES

Delicious nymph, suppose there were
Nor honour nor report,
Yet manliness would scorn to wear
The time in idle sport;
 For toil doth give a better touch
To make us feel our joy,
And ease finds tediousness as much
As labour yields annoy.

SIREN

Then pleasure likewise seems the shore
Whereto tends all your toil,
Which you forgo to make it more,
And perish oft the while.
 Who may disport them diversely
Find never tedious day,
And ease may have variety
As well as action may.

ULYSSES

But natures of the noblest frame
These toils and dangers please;
And they take comfort in the same
As much as you in ease;
 And with the thought of actions past
Are recreated still;
When Pleasure leaves a touch at last
To shew that it was ill.

Siren

That doth *Opinion* only cause
That's out of *Custom* bred,
Which makes us many other laws
Than ever *Nature* did.
    No widows wail for our delights,
Our sports are without blood;
The world we see by warlike wights
Receives more hurt than good.

Ulysses

But yet the state of things require
These motions of unrest;
And these great spirits of high desire
Seem born to turn them best;
    To purge the mischiefs that increase
And all good order mar,
For oft we see a wicked peace
To be well changed for war.

Siren

Well, well, Ulysses, then I see
I shall not have thee here;
And therefore I will come to thee
And take my fortune there.
    I must be won that cannot win
Yet lost were I not won,
For beauty hath created been
To undo, or be undone.

From THE QUEEN'S ARCADIA

Beauty

Something there is peculiar and alone
To every beauty, that doth give an edge
To our desires, and more we will conceive
In that we have not, than in that we have.
And I have heard abroad, where best experience
And wit is learned, that all the fairest choice
Of women in the world serve but to make
One perfect beauty, whereof each brings part.
One hath a pleasing smile, and nothing else:
Another but some silly mole to grace
The area of a disproportioned face;
Another pleases not but when she speaks,
And some in silence only graceful are:
Some till they laugh, we see, seem to be fair;
Some have their bodies good, their gestures ill,
Some please in motion, some in sitting still;
Some are thought lovely that have nothing fair,
Some again fair that nothing lovely are.
So that we see how beauty doth consist
Of divers pieces, and yet all attract.
                    (Act ii. Scene iii.)

From TETHYS' FESTIVAL

Pleasure and Imagination

Are they shadows that we see?
And can shadows pleasure give?
Pleasures only shadows be,
Cast by bodies we conceive,
And are made the things we deem
In those figures which they seem.

But these pleasures vanish fast,
Which by shadows are exprest;
Pleasures are not, if they last;
In their passing is their best.
Glory is most bright and gay
In a flash and so away.

Feed apace, then, greedy eyes
On the wonder you behold;
Take it sudden as it flies,
Though you take it not to hold.
When your eyes have done their part,
Thought must length it in the heart.

From HYMEN'S TRIUMPH

Thirsis Describes His First Love for Silvia

Ah, I remember well (and how can I
But evermore remember well) when first
Our flame began, when scarce we knew what was
The flame we felt; when as we sat and sighed
And looked upon each other, and conceived
Not what we ailed, yet something we did ail;
And yet were well, and yet we were not well;
And what was our disease we could not tell.
Then would we kiss, then sigh, then look: And thus
In that first garden of our simpleness
We spent our childhood: but when years began
To reap the fruit of knowledge, ah, how then
Would she with graver looks, with sweet stern brow,
Check my presumption and my forwardness;
Yet still would give me flowers, still would me show
What she would have me, yet not have me, know.

Thirsis' Song

Eyes hide my love and do not show
   To any but to her my notes,
Who only doth that cipher know,
   Wherewith we pass our secret thoughts:
Bely your looks in others' sight;
   And wrong yourselves to do her right.

Chorus.

 Love is a sickness full of woes
  All remedies refusing :
 A plant that with most cutting grows,
  Most barren with best using.
   Why so ?
 More we enjoy it, more it dies;
  If not enjoyed, it sighing cries
   Heyho.

 Love is a torment of the mind,
  A tempest everlasting :
 And Jove hath made it of a kind,
  Not well, nor full, nor fasting.
   Why so ?
 More we enjoy it, more it dies,
  If not enjoyed, it sighing cries
   Heyho.

The Recovery of Thirsis and Silvia

Good news, my friends, and I will tell it you!
Silvia and Thirsis being to my cottage brought,
The skilful Lamia comes and searched the wound
Which Silvia had received of this rude swain.
And finding it not deadly, she applied
Those remedies she knew of best effect.
And binds it up and pours into her mouth
Such cordial waters as revive the spirits:
And so much wrought, as she at length perceived
Life was not quite gone out, but lay oppressed.
 With like endeavours we on Thirsis work,
And ministered like cordials unto him :
At length we might hear Silvia fetch a groan,
And therewithal Thirsis perceived to move;

Then Thirsis fetched a groan, and Silvia moved,
As if their lives were made both of one piece.
Whereat we joyed and then removed, and set
Each before other, and held up their heads,
And chafed their temples, rubbed and stroked their
    cheeks.
  Wherewith first Silvia cast up her dim eyes
And presently did Thirsis lift up his.
And then again they both together sighed
And each on other fixed an unseeing eye:
For yet 'twas scarce the twilight of their new
Returning day, out of the night of death.
And though they saw, they did not yet perceive
Each other, and yet both turned to one point,
As touched alike, and held their looks direct.
At length we might perceive, as life began
To appear, and make the morning in their eyes;
Their beams were clearer, and their opener looks
Did shew as if they took some little note
Of each the other: yet not so as they
Could thoroughly discern who themselves were.
  And then we took and joined their hands in one,
And held them so a while, until we felt
How ev'n each other's touch the motion gave
Unto their feeling, and they trembling wrung
Their hands together, and so held them locked,
Looked still upon each other, but no words at all.
  Then we called out to Thirsis, "Thirsis, look,
It is thy Silvia thou here hold'st, she is
Returned, revived, and safe; Silvia, behold thou hast
Thy Thirsis, and shalt ever have him thine."
  Then did we set them both upon their feet
And there they stood in act, ev'n as before,
Looking upon each other, hand in hand:

At last we saw a blushing red appear
In both their cheeks, which sense set as a lamp
To light their understanding. And forthwith
The tears gushed forth their eyes, which hindered
            them
A while from seeing each other, till they had
Cleared them again. And then as if new waked
From out a fearful dream, they stand and doubt
Whether they were awake indeed, or else
Still in a dream, distrusting their own eyes.
Their long-endured miseries would not
Let them believe their sudden happiness
Although they saw it : till with much ado
They had confirmed their credit, and had kissed
Each other, and embraced, and kissed again,
And yet still dumb ; their joy now seemed to be
Too busy with their thoughts, to allow them words.

 And then they walked a little, then stood still,
Then walked again, and still held other fast,
As if they feared they should be lost again.

 And when at last they spake, it was but this,
O Silvia and *O Thirsis,* and there stopped.

 We, lest our sight and presence (being there
So many) hinder might the passage of
Their modest, simple and unpractised love,
Came all our way, and only Lamia left,
Whose spirit, and that sufficient skill she hath,
Will serve, no doubt, to see they shall do well.

AN ODE

Now each creature joys the other
    Passing happy days and hours,
One bird reports unto another
    In the fall of silver showers,
Whilst the earth (our common mother)
    Hath her bosom decked with flowers.

Whilst the greatest torch of heaven,
    With bright rays warms Flora's lap,
Making nights and days both even,
    Cheering plants with fresher sap;
My field, of flowers quite bereaven,
    Wants refresh of better hap.

Echo, daughter of the Air,
    Babbling guest of rocks and hills,
Knows the name of my fierce Fair,
    And sounds the accents of my ills.
Each thing pities my despair,
    Whilst that she her lover kills.

An Ode

Whilst that she, O cruel maid,
   Doth me and my [1] love despise,
My life's flourish is decayed
   That depended on her eyes:
But her will must be obeyed,
   And well he ends for love who dies.

[1] First edition reads *my true love*.

Lux Hareshulla tibi (Warwici villa, tenebris
Ante tuas Cunas, obsita) Prima fuit.
Arma, Viros, Veneres, Patriam modulamine dixti:
Te Patria resonant Arma, Viri, Veneres.

A SELECTION FROM THE POEMS OF MICHAEL DRAYTON

From THE NINTH ECLOGUE

DAFFADILL

Batte. Gorbo as thou cam'st this way
By yonder little hill,
Or as thou through the fields didst stray
Saw'st thou my Daffadill?

She's in a frock of Lincoln green,
Which colour likes her sight,
And never hath her beauty seen
But through a veil of white.

Than roses richer to behold
That trim up lovers' bowers,
The pansy and the marigold,
Though Phœbus' paramours.

Gorbo. Thou well describ'st the daffadill;
      It is not full an hour
      Since by the spring near yonder hill
      I saw that lovely flower.

Batte. Yet my fair flower thou didst not meet
      Nor news of her didst bring,
      And yet my Daffadill's more sweet
      Than that by yonder spring.

Gorbo. I saw a shepherd, that doth keep
      In yonder field of lilies,
      Was making (as he fed his sheep)
      A wreath of daffadilies.

Batte. Yet, Gorbo, thou delud'st me still;
      My flower thou didst not see,
      For, know, my pretty Daffadill
      Is worn of none but me.

      To show itself but near her feet
      No lily is so bold,
      Except to shade her from the heat
      Or keep her from the cold.

Gorbo. Through yonder vale as I did pass,
      Descending from the hill,
      I met a smirking bonny lass;
      They call her Daffadill.

      Whose presence as along she went
      The pretty flowers did greet
      As though their heads they downward bent
      With homage to her feet.

Daffadill

      And all the shepherds that were nigh
      From top of every hill
      Unto the valleys loud did cry
      " There goes sweet Daffadill."

Batte. Ay, gentle shepherd, now with joy
      Thou all my flocks dost fill;
      That's she alone, kind shepherd's boy;
      Let us to Daffadill.

From ENDYMION AND PHŒBE

Diana's Grove at Latmos

Upon this mount there stood a stately grove,
Whose reaching arms to clip the welkin strove,
Of tufted Cedars and the branching Pine
Whose bushy tops themselves do so entwine
As seemed when Nature first this work begun
She then conspired against the piercing Sun:
Under whose covert thus divinely made
Phœbus' green Laurel flourished in the shade,
Fair Venus' Myrtle, Mars' his warlike Fir,
Minerva's Olive, and the weeping Myrrh,
The patient Palm which thrives in spite of hate,
The Poplar to Apollo consecrate.
Which Nature in such order had disposed,
And therewithal these goodly walks enclosed,
As served for hangings and rich tapestry
To beautify this stately gallery.
Embroidring these in curious trails along
The clustred grapes, the golden citrons hung;
More glorious than the precious fruit were these
Kept by the dragon in Hesperides,
Or gorgeous arras in rich colours wrought
With silk from Afric or from India brought.
Out of this soil sweet bubbling fountains crept,
As though for joy the senseless stones had wept;

With straying channels dancing sundry ways,
With often turns, like to a curious maze;
Which breaking forth the tender grass bedewed,
Whose silver sand with orient pearl was strewed;
Shadowed with roses and sweet eglantine
Dipping their sprays into this crystalline;
From which the birds the purple berries pruned
And to their loves their small recorders tuned;
The nightingale, wood's herald of the spring,
The whistling ousel, mavis carolling,
Tuning their trebles to the water's fall;—
Which made the music more angelical.
Whilst gentle zephyr, murmuring among,
Kept time, and bare the burden to the song.

From ENGLAND'S HEROICAL EPISTLES

CHARLES BRANDON, DUKE OF SUFFOLK, TO MARY, THE FRENCH QUEEN

BUT that my faith commands me to forbear,
The fault's your own if I impatient were;
Were my despatch such as should be my speed,
I should want time your loving lines to read.
Here in the Court, chameleon-like I fare,
And as that creature only feed on air.
All day I wait and all the night I watch,
And starve mine ears to hear of my despatch.
    If Dover were th' Abydos of my rest,
Or pleasant Calais were my Mary's Sest,
You should not need, bright Queen, to blame me so,
Did not the distance to desire say *no*;
No tedious night from travel should be free,
Till through the seas, with swimming still to thee,
A snowy path I made unto thy bay
So bright as is that nectar-stained way
The restless sun by travelling doth wear
Passing his course to finish up the year.
But Paris locks my love within the main,
And London yet thy Brandon doth detain.
    Of thy firm love thou put'st me still in mind,
But of my faith not one word can I find.

When Longaville to Mary was affied
And thou by him wast made King Lewis' bride,
Oft have I wished that thou a prize might'st be
That I in arms might combat him for thee!
And in the madness of my love distraught
A thousand times his murder have forethought
But that th' all-seeing Powers, which sit above,
Regard not madmen's oaths, nor faults in love;
And have confirmed it by the grant of heaven
That lovers' sins on earth should be forgiven.
For never man is half so much distressed
As he that loves, to see his love possessed.
  Coming to Richmond after thy depart,
Richmond where first thou stol'st away my heart,
Methought it looked not as it did of late,
But, wanting thee, forlorn and desolate;
In whose fair walks thou often hast been seen
To sport with Kath'rine, Henry's beauteous queen,
Astonishing sad winter with thy sight,
So that for thee the day hath put back night;
And the small birds, as in the pleasant spring,
Forget themselves and have begun to sing.
  So oft as I by Thames go and return
Methinks for thee the river yet doth mourn;
Whom I have seen to let his stream at large
Which, like an handmaid, waited on thy barge,
And if thou hap'st against the flood to row,
Which way it ebb'd it presently would flow,
Weeping in drops upon the labouring oars
For joy that it had got thee from the shores.
The swans, with music that the rudders make,
Ruffling their plumes came gliding on the lake,
As the swift dolphins by Arion's strings
Were brought to land with siren ravishings.

The flocks and herds that pasture near the flood
To gaze on thee have oft forborne their food,
And sat down sadly mourning by the brim
That they by nature were not made to swim.

. . . . . .

How should I joy of thy arrive to hear?
But as a poor sea-faring passenger
After long travel, tempest-torn and wracked,
By some unpitying pirate that is sacked,
Hears the false robber that hath stol'n his wealth
Landed in some safe harbour, and in health,
Enriched with the invaluable store
For which he long had travelled before!

. . . . . .

When Marquess Dorset and the valiant Grays
To purchase fame first crossed the narrow seas,
With all the knights that my associates went
In honour of thy nuptial tournament,
Think'st thou I joy'd not in thy beauty's pride
When thou in triumph did'st through Paris ride,
Where all the streets as thou did'st pass along
With arras, biss, and tapestry was hung?
Ten thousand gallant citizens prepared
In rich attire thy princely self to guard:
Next them, three thousand choice religious men
In golden vestments followed on agen,
And in procession as they came along
With *Hymen* sweetly sang the marriage song:
Next these, five Dukes, as did their places fall,
With each of them a princely Cardinal:
Then thou, on thy imperial chariot set,
Crowned with a rich impearled coronet;
Whilst the Parisian dames, as thy train past,
Their precious incense in abundance cast.

As Cynthia, from her wave-embattled shrouds,
Opening the west, comes streaming through the clouds,
With shining troops of silver-tressed stars
Attending on her as her torch-bearers;
And all the lesser lights about her throne
With admiration stand as lookers-on;
Whilst she alone in height of all her pride
The Queen of Light along her sphere doth glide.
    When on the tilt my horse like thunder came
No other signal had I but thy name;
Thy voice my trumpet and my guide thine eyes,
And but thy beauty I esteemed no prize.
That large-limbed Almain of the Giant's race,
Which bare strength on his breast, fear in his face,
Whose sinewed arms with his steel-tempered blade
Through plate and mail such open passage made,
Upon whose might the Frenchmen's glory lay,
And all the hope of that victorious day;
Thou saw'st thy Brandon beat him on his knee,
Offering his shield a conquered spoil to thee.
But thou wilt say perhaps, I vainly boast
And tell thee that which thou already know'st.
No, sacred Queen, my valour I deny,
It was thy beauty not my chivalry.
One of thy tressed curls there falling down
As loath to be imprisoned in thy crown,
I saw the soft air sportively to take it,
And into strange and sundry forms to make it;
Now parting it to four, to three, to twain,
Now twisting it, then it untwist again;
Then make the threads to dally with thine eye,
A sunny candle for a golden fly.

E

At length from thence one little tear it got,
Which falling down as though a star had shot,
My up-turned eye pursued it with my sight,
The which again redoubled all my might.
  'Tis but in vain of my descent to boast;
When Heaven's lamp shines, all other lights be lost.
Falcons seem poor, the eagle sitting by,
Whose brood surveys the sun with open eye.
Else might my blood find issue from his force
Who beat the tyrant Richard from his horse
On Bosworth plain, whom Richmond chose to wield
His glorious ensign in that conquering field;
And with his sword, in his dear sovereign's fight,
To his last breath stood fast in Henry's right.
  Then, beauteous Empress, think this safe delay
Shall be the even to a joyful day.
Foresight doth still on all advantage lie;
Wise men must give place to necessity;
To put back ill our good we must forbear;
Better first fear than after still to fear.
'Twere oversight in that, at which we aim,
To put the hazard on an after-game;
With patience then let us our hopes attend;
And, till I come, receive these lines I send.

A PASSION OF KING HENRY TO FAIR ROSAMOND

Fatal my birth, unfortunate my life,
Unkind my children, most unkind my wife.
Grief, cares, old age, suspicion, to torment me;
Nothing on earth to quiet or content me;
So many woes, so many plagues to find—
Sickness of body, discontent of mind.

Hopes left, helps reft, life wronged, joy interdicted,
Banished, distressed, forsaken and afflicted.
Of all relief hath Fortune quite bereft me;
Only my love yet to my comfort left me.
And is one beauty thought so great a thing
To mitigate the sorrows of a king?
Barred of that choice the vulgar often prove,
Have we than they less privilege in love?
Is it a king the woful widow hears?
Is it a king dries up the orphan's tears?
Is it a king regards the client's cry?
Gives life to him by law condemned to die?
Is it his care the commonwealth that keeps,
As doth the nurse her baby whilst it sleeps?—
And that poor king of all those hopes prevented,
Unheard, unhelped, unpitied, unlamented!
    Yet let me be with poverty oppressed,
Of earthly blessings robbed and dispossessed,
Let me be scorned, rejected, and reviled,
And from my kingdom let me live exiled;
Let the world's curse upon me still remain,
And let the last bring on the first again,
All miseries that wretched man may wound;—
Leave for my comfort only Rosamund.
Thy presence hath repaired in one day
What many years with sorrow did decay,
And made fresh beauty in her flower to spring
Out of the wrinkles of Time's ruining.
Even as the hungry winter-starved earth
When she by nature labours towards her birth,
Still as the day upon the dark world creeps,
One blossom forth after another peeps,
Till the small flower, whose root at last unbound
Gets from the frosty prison of the ground,

Spreading the leaves unto the powerful noon,
Decked in fresh colours smiles upon the sun.

PRINCES LIKE SUNS

Princes, like suns, be evermore in sight;
All see the clouds betwixt them and their light;
Yet they which lighten all, down from their skies,
See not the clouds offending others' eyes..
And deem their noontide is desired of all,
When all expect clear changes from their fall.

LOVE'S SEPTEMBER

MY breast which once was mirth's imperial throne
A vast and desert wilderness is grown:
Like that cold region from the world remote,
On whose breem seas the icy mountains float;
Where those poor creatures, banished from the light,
Do live imprisoned in continual night.
No object greets my soul's internal eyes
But divinations of sad tragedies;
And care takes up her solitary inn
Where youth and joy their court did once begin.
As in September, when our year resigns
The glorious sun to the cold watery signs
Which through the clouds looks on the earth in
    scorn,
The little bird yet to salute the morn
Upon the naked branches sets her foot,
The leaves then lying on the mossy root,
And there a silly chirriping doth keep
As though she fain would sing, yet fain would weep,
Praising fair summer that too soon is gone,
Or sad for Winter too fast coming on:
In this strange plight I mourn for thy depart
Because that weeping cannot ease my heart.

THE TOWER OF MORTIMER
From the Barons' Wars

WITHIN the Castle had the Queen devised,
Long about which she busied had her thought,
A chamber, wherein she imparadised
What shapes for her could anywhere be sought;
Which in the same were curiously comprised,
By skilful painters excellently wrought:
    And in the place of greatest safety there,
    Which she had named the Tower of Mortimer.

A room prepared with pilasters she chose,
That to the roof their slender points did rear,
Arching the top, whereas they all did close,
Which from below showed like an hemisphere;
In whose concavity she did compose
The constellations that to us appear
    In their corporeal shapes, with stars enchased,
    As by the old poets they on Heaven were placed.

About which lodging, towards the upper face,
Ran a fine border, circularly led,
As equal 'twixt the zenith and the base,
Which as a zone the waist engirdléd,
That lent the sight a breathing, by the space
'Twixt things near hand and those far overhead,
    Upon the plain wall of which lower part
    Painting expressed the utmost of her art.

There Phœbus clipping Hyacinthus stood,
Whose life's last drops did the god's breast imbrue,
His tears so mixéd with the young boy's blood,
That whether was the more no eye could view;
And though together lost as in a flood,
Yet here and there the one from the other drew:
   The pretty wood-nymphs chafing him with balm,
   Proving to wake him from his deadly qualm.

Apollo's quiver and far-killing bow,
His gold-fringed mantle on the grassful ground,
To express whose act Art even her best did show,
The sledge so shadowed still as to rebound,
As it had scarce done giving of the blow,
Lending a lasting freshness to the wound;
   The purple flower from the boy's blood begun,
   That since ne'er spreads but to the rising sun.

There Mercury was like a shepherd's boy,
Sporting with Hebe by a fountain brim,
With many a sweet glance, many an amorous toy;
He sprinkling drops at her, and she at him:
Wherein the painter so explained their joy
As he had meant the very life to limn:
   For on their brows he made the drops so clear
   That through each drop their fair skins did appear.

By them in landscape rocky Cynthus reared,
With the clouds leaning on his lofty crown,
On his sides showing many a straggling herd,
And from his top the clear springs creeping down
By the old rocks, each with a hoary beard,
With moss and climbing ivy overgrown:

The Tower of Mortimer

So done that the beholders with the skill
Never enough their longing eyes could fill.

The half-naked nymphs, some climbing, some
  descending,
The sundry flowers at one another flung,
In postures strange their limber bodies bending;
Some cropping branches that seemed lately sprung,
Upon the brakes their coloured mantles rending,
Which on the mount grew here and there among;
  Combing their hair some, some made garlands by:
  So strove the painter to content the eye.

In one part, Phaëton cast amongst the clouds
By Phœbus' palfreys, that their reins had broke,
His chariot tumbling from the welkéd shrouds,
And the fierce steeds flew madding from their yoke;
The elements confusedly in crowds,
And heaven and earth were nought but flame and
  smoke;
  A piece so done that many did desire
  To warm themselves, some frighted with the fire.

And for the light to this brave lodging lent,
The workman, who as wisely could direct,
Did for the same the windows so invent
That they should artificially reflect
The day alike on every lineament
To their proportion, and had such respect
  As that the beams, condensated and grave,
  To every figure a sure colour gave.

In part of which, under a golden vine,
Which held a curious canopy through all,

Stood a rich bed, quite covered with the twine,
Shadowing the same in the redoubling fall,
Whose clusters drew the branches to decline,
'Mongst which did many a naked Cupid sprawl:
    Some at the sundry-coloured birds did shoot,
    And some about to pluck the purple fruit.

On which a tissue counterpane was cast,
Arachne's web did not the same surpass,
Wherein the story of his fortunes past
In lively pictures neatly handled was,—
How he escaped the Tower, in France how graced,—
With stones embroidered of a wondrous mass;
    About the border, in a fine-wrought fret,
    Emblems, impresses, hieroglyphics set.

This flattering sunshine had begot the shower,
And the black clouds with such abundance fed,
That for a wind they waited but the hour
With force to let their fury on his head;
Which when it came, it came with such a power
As he could hardly have imagined:
    But when men think they most in safety stand,
    Their greatest peril often is at hand.

For to that largeness they increaséd were,
That Edward felt March heavy on his throne,
Whose props no longer both of them could bear,
Two for one seat that over-great were grown,
Preposterously that movéd in one sphere,
And to the like predominancy prone,
    That the young King down Mortimer must cast,
    If he himself would e'er hope to sit fast.

Who finding the necessity was such
That urged him still the assault to undertake,
And yet his person it might nearly touch
Should he too soon his sleeping power awake;
The attempt, wherein the danger was so much,
Drove him at length a secret means to make
    Whereby he might the enterprise effect,
    And hurt him most where he did least suspect.

Without the castle, in the earth is found
A cave, resembling sleepy Morpheus' cell,
In strange meanders winding underground,
Where darkness seeks continually to dwell,
Which with such fear and horror doth abound
As though it were an entrance into hell:
    By architects to serve the castle made
    Whenas the Danes this island did invade.

Now, on along the crankling path doth keep,
Then by a rock turns up another way,
Rising towards day, then falling towards the deep,
On a smooth level then itself doth lay,
Directly then, then obliquely doth creep,
Nor in the course keeps any certain stay,
    Till in the castle, in an odd by-place,
    It casts the foul mask from its dusky face.

By which the King, with a selected crew
Of such as he with his intent acquainted,
Which he affected to the action knew,
And in revenge of Edward had not fainted,
That to their utmost would the cause pursue,
And with those treasons that had not been tainted,
    Adventuréd the labyrinth to essay,
    To rouse the beast which kept them all at bay.

Long after Phœbus took his labouring team
To his pale sister and resigned his place,
To wash his cauples in the ocean stream,
And cool the fervour of his glowing face ;
And Phœbe, scanted of her brother's beam,
Into the West went after him apace,
 Leaving black darkness to possess the sky,
 To fit the time of that black tragedy.

What time by torchlight they attempt the cave,
Which at their entrance seeméd in a fright
With the reflection that their armour gave,
As it till then had ne'er seen any light ;
Which striving their pre-eminence to have,
Darkness therewith so daringly doth fight
 That each confounding other, both appear
 As darkness light, and light but darkness were.

And by the lights as they along were led,
Their shadows then them following at their back,
Were like to mourners carrying forth their dead,
And as the deed so were they ugly black,
Or like the fiends that them had followéd,
Pricking them on to bloodshed and to wrack ;
 Whilst the light looked as it had been amazed
 At their deforméd shapes whereon it gazed.

The night waxed old (not dreaming of these
  things),
And to her chamber is the Queen withdrawn,
To whom a choice musician plays and sings
Whilst she sat under an estate of lawn,
In night attire more godlike glittering
Than any eye had seen the cheerful dawn,

The Tower of Mortimer

Leaning upon her most loved Mortimer,
Whose voice, more than the music, pleased her ear.

Where her fair breasts at liberty were let,
Whose violet veins in branchéd riverets flow,
And Venus' swans and milky doves were set
Upon those swelling mounts of driven snow;
Whereon, whilst Love to sport himself doth get,
He lost his way, nor back again could go,
But with those banks of beauty set about
He wandered still, yet never could get out.

Her loose hair looked like gold (O word too base!
Nay, more than sin but so to name her hair)
Declining, as to kiss her fairer face,
No word is fair enough for thing so fair,
Nor ever was there epithet could grace
That by much praising which we much impair;
And where the pen fails, pencils cannot show it,
Only the soul may be supposed to know it.

She laid her fingers on his manly cheek,
The god's pure sceptres and the darts of love,
That with their touch might make a tiger meek
Or might great Atlas from his seat remove;
So white, so soft, so delicate, so sleek,
As she had worn a lily for a glove,
As might beget life where was never none,
And put a spirit into the hardest stone.

The fire of precious wood, the light perfume,
Which left a sweetness on each thing it shone,

As everything did to itself assume
The scent from them, and made the same their own:
So that the painted flowers within the room
Were sweet, as if they naturally had grown;
    The light gave colours which upon them fell,
    And to the colours the perfume gave smell.

  When on those sundry pictures they devise,
And from one piece they to another run,
Commend that face, that arm, that hand, those eyes,
Show how that bird, how well that flower was done,
How this part shadowed, and how that did rise,
This top was clouded, how that trail was spun,
    The landscape, mixture, and delineatings.
    And in that art a thousand curious things.

  Looking upon proud Phaëton wrapped in fire,
The gentle Queen did much bewail his fall;
But Mortimer commended his desire
To lose one poor life or to govern all:
"What though," quoth he, "he madly did aspire,
And his great mind made him proud Fortune's
    thrall?
    Yet in despite, when she her worst had done,
    He perished in the chariot of the sun."

  When by that time into the Castle hall
Was rudely entered that well-arméd rout,
And they within suspecting nought at all,
Had then no guard to watch for them without:
See how mischances suddenly do fall,
And steal upon us, being farth'st from doubt:
    Our life's uncertain and our death is sure,
    And towards most peril man is most secure.

IDEA

If chaste and pure devotion of my youth,
Or glory of my April-springing years,
Unfeigned love in naked, simple truth,
A thousand vows, a thousand sighs and tears;
Or if a world of faithful service done,
Words, thoughts, and deeds devoted to her honour,
Or eyes that have beheld her as their sun,
With admiration ever looking on her;
A life that never joyed but in her love,
A soul that ever hath adored her name,
A faith that Time nor Fortune could not move,
A Muse that unto heaven hath raised her fame;
    Though these, nor these, deserve to be embraced,
    Yet, fair unkind, too good to be disgraced.

My heart was slain, and none but you and I;
Who should I think the murder should commit
Since but yourself there was no creature by,
But only I, guiltless of murdering it.
It slew itself; the verdict on the view
Do quit the dead, and me not accessory:
Well, well, I fear it will be proved by you,
The evidence so great a proof doth carry.
But O, see, see, we need enquire no further,
Upon your lips the scarlet drops are found,

And in your eye the boy that did the murder,
Your cheeks yet pale, since first he gave the wound.
    By this I see, however things be past,
    Yet Heaven will still have murder out at last.

Nothing but No and I,[1] and I and No:
How falls it out so strangely you reply?
I tell you, fair, I'll not be answered so,
With this affirming No, denying I.
I say, I love, you slightly answer I:
I say, you love, you pule me out a No:
I say, I die, you echo me with I:
Save me! I cry, you sigh me out a No.
Must woe and I have nought but No and I?
No, I am I, if I no more can have;
Answer no more, with silence make reply,
And let me take myself what I do crave:
    Let No and I with I and you be so:
    Then answer No and I, and I and No.

How many paltry, foolish, painted things
That now in coaches trouble every street,
Shall be forgotten, whom no poet sings,
Ere they be well wrapped in their winding-sheet?
Where I to thee eternity shall give
When nothing else remaineth of these days,
And Queens hereafter shall be glad to live
Upon the alms of thy superfluous praise.
Virgins and matrons reading these my rhymes,
Shall be so much delighted with thy story,
That they shall grieve they lived not in these times,
To have seen thee, their sex's only glory:
    So shalt thou fly above the vulgar throng,
    Still to survive in my immortal song.

    [1] *i.e.,* aye.

To nothing fitter can I thee compare
Than to the son of some rich penny-father,
Who having now brought on his end with care,
Leaves to his son all he had heaped together;
This new rich novice, lavish of his chest,
To one man gives, doth on another spend,
Then here he riots, yet amongst the rest
Haps to lend some to one true honest friend.
Thy gifts thou in obscurity dost waste,
False friends thy kindness, born but to deceive thee;
Thy love, that is on the unworthy placed;
Time hath thy beauty, which with age will leave thee;
   Only that little which to me was lent
   I give thee back when all the rest is spent.

If he from Heaven that filched that living fire
Condemned by Jove to endless torment be,
I greatly marvel how you still go free
That far beyond Prometheus did aspire:
The fire he stole, although of heavenly kind,
Which from above he craftily did take,
Of lifeless clods us living men to make,
He did bestow in temper of the mind:
But you broke into Heaven's immortal store,
Where virtue, honour, wit, and beauty lay;
Which taking thence you have escaped away,
Yet stand as free as e'er you did before;
   Yet old Prometheus punished for his rape:
   Thus poor thieves suffer when the greater scape.

Idea

To Time

Stay, speedy Time, behold before thou pass,
From age to age what thou hast sought to see,
One in whom all the excellences be,
In whom Heaven looks itself as in a glass;
Time, look thou too in this translucent glass,
And thy youth past in this pure mirror see,
As the world's beauty in his infancy,
What it was then, and thou before it was.
Pass on, and to posterity tell this,
Yet see thou tell but truly what hath been;
Say to our nephews that thou once hast seen
In perfect human shape all heavenly bliss;
    And bid them mourn, nay more, despair with
        thee,
    That she is gone, her like again to see.

The glorious Sun went blushing to his bed;
When my soul's sun from her fair cabinet
Her golden beams had now discovered,
Lightening the world eclipsed by his set.
Some mused to see the earth envy the air,
Which from her lips exhaled refined sweet;
A world to see, yet how he joyed to hear
The dainty grass make music with her feet.
But my most marvel was when from the skies
So comet-like each star advanced her light,
As though the heaven had now awaked her eyes,
And summoned angels to this blessed sight.
    No cloud was seen, but crystalline the air,
    Laughing for joy upon my lovely fair.

To Humour

You cannot love, my pretty heart, and why?
There was a time you told me that you would:
But now again you will the same deny,
If it might please you, would to God you could.
What, will you hate? nay, that you will not neither;
Nor love, nor hate, how then? what will you do?
What, will you keep a mean then betwixt either?
Or will you love me, and yet hate me too?
Yet serves not this: what next, what other shift?
You will and will not, what a coil is here!
I see your craft now I perceive your drift,
And all this while I was mistaken there;
    Your love and hate is this, I now do prove you,
    You love in hate, by hate to make me love you.

Love, banished Heaven, in earth was held in scorn,
Wandering abroad in need and beggary;
And wanting friends, though of a goddess born,
Yet craved the alms of such as passéd by:
I, like a man devout and charitable,
Clothéd the naked, lodged this wandering guest,
With sighs and tears still furnishing his table,
With what might make the miserable blest;
But this ungrateful, for my good desert,
Enticed my thoughts against me to conspire,
Who gave consent to steal away my heart,
And set my breast, his lodging, on a fire.
    Well, well, my friends, when beggars grow thus bold,
    No marvel then though charity grow cold.

I hear some say, "This man is not in love:
Who can he love? a likely thing," they say;
"Read but his verse, and it will easily prove."
O, judge not rashly, gentle Sir, I pray.
Because I loosely trifle in this sort
As one that fain his sorrows would beguile,
You now suppose me all this time in sport,
And please yourself with this conceit the while.
Ye shallow censures, sometimes see ye not
In greatest perils some men pleasant be,
Where fame by death is only to be got,
They resolute? So stands the case with me;
 Where other men in depth of passion cry,
 I laugh at Fortune, as in jest to die.

To the Senses

When conquering love did first my heart assail,
Unto mine aid I summoned every sense,
Doubting, if that proud tyrant should prevail,
My heart should suffer for mine eyes' offence;
But he with beauty first corrupted sight,
My hearing bribed with her tongue's harmony,
My taste by her sweet lips drawn with delight,
My smelling won with her breath's spicery:
But when my touching came to play his part
(The king of senses, greater than the rest),
He yields love up the keys unto my heart,
And tells the other how they should be blest:
 And thus by those of whom I hoped for aid,
 To cruel love my soul was first betrayed.

Idea

To Miracle

Some, misbelieving and profane in love,
When I do speak of miracles by thee,
May say that thou art flatteréd by me,
Who only write my skill in verse to prove ;
See miracles, ye unbelieving, see,
A dumb-born Muse made to express the mind,
A cripple hand to write, yet lame by kind,
One by thy name, the other touching thee ;
Blind were mine eyes till they were seen of thine,
And mine ears deaf, by thy fame healéd be,
My vices cured by virtues sprung from thee,
My hopes revived, which long in grave had lain :
    All unclean thoughts, foul spirits, cast out in me,
    Only by virtue that proceeds from thee.

Cupid Conjured

Thou purblind boy, since thou hast been so slack
To wound her heart whose eyes have wounded me,
And suffered her to glory in my wrack,
Thus to my aid I lastly conjure thee ;
By hellish Styx, by which the Thunderer swears,
By thy fair mother's unavoided power,
By Hecate's names, by Proserpine's sad tears
When she was rapt to the infernal bower ;
By thine own lovéd Psyche, by the fires
Spent on thine altars, flaming up to Heaven ;
By all true lovers' sighs, vows, and desires,
By all the wounds that ever thou hast given ;
    I conjure thee by all that I have named
    To make her love, or Cupid, be thou damned.

Dear, why should you command me to my rest,
When now the night doth summon all to sleep?
Methinks this time becometh lovers best;
Night was ordained together friends to keep:
How happy are all other living things,
Which though the day disjoin by several flight,
The quiet evening yet together brings,
And each returns unto his love at night?
O thou that art so courteous else to all,
Why shouldst thou, Night, abuse me only thus,
That every creature to his kind dost call,
And yet 'tis thou dost only sever us?
    Well could I wish it would be ever day,
    If, when night comes, you bid me go away.

Why should your fair eyes with such sovereign grace
Disperse their rays on every vulgar spirit,
Whilst I in darkness in the self-same place
Get not one glance to recompense my merit?
So doth the ploughman gaze the wandering star,
And only rest contented with the light,
That never learned what constellations are,
Beyond the bent of his unknowing sight.
O, why should beauty, custom to obey,
To their gross sense apply herself so ill!
Would God I were as ignorant as they,
When I am made unhappy by my skill;
    Only compelled on this poor good to boast,
    Heavens are not kind to them that know them most.

Plain-pathed Experience, the unlearnéd's guide,
Her simple followers evidently shows

Idea

Sometimes what schoolmen scarcely can decide,
Nor yet wise reason absolutely knows:
In making trial of a murder wrought,
If the vile actors of the heinous deed
Near the dead body happily be brought,
Oft 't hath been proved the breathless corse will
    bleed;
She coming near, that my poor heart hath slain,
Long since departed, to the world no more,
The ancient wounds no longer can contain,
But fall to bleeding, as they did before:
    But what of this? Should she to death be led,
    It furthers justice, but helps not the dead.

Thou leaden brain, which censurest what I write,
And sayst my lines be dull and do not move;
I marvel not thou feel'st not my delight,
Which never felt'st my fiery touch of love,
But thou, whose pen hath like a pack-horse served,
Whose stomach unto gall hath turned thy food,
Whose senses, like poor prisoners, hunger-starved,
Whose grief hath parched thy body, dried thy blood;
Thou which hast scornéd life and hated death,
And in a moment mad, sober, glad, and sorry:
Thou which hast banned thy thoughts, and cursed
    thy birth
With thousand plagues more than in Purgatory:
    Thou, thus whose spirit Love in his fire refines,
    Come thou and read, admire, applaud my lines.

As in some countries far remote from hence,
The wretched creature destinéd to die,
Having the judgment due to his offence,
By surgeons begged, their art on him to try,

Which on the living work without remorse,
First make incision on each mastering vein,
Then stanch the bleeding, then transpierce the corse,
And with their balms recure the wounds again,
Then poison and with physic him restore:
Not that they fear the hopeless man to kill,
But their experience to increase the more:
Even so my mistress works upon my ill;
   By curing me and killing me each hour,
   Only to show her beauty's sovereign power.

To Proverb

As Love and I late harboured in one inn,
With proverbs thus each other entertain;
"In love there is no lack," thus I begin;
"Fair words make fools," replieth he again:
"Who spares to speak doth spare to speed," quoth I;
"As well," saith he, "too forward as too slow":
"Fortune assists the boldest," I reply;
"A hasty man," quoth he, "ne'er wanted woe":
"Labour is light where love," quoth I, "doth pay";
Saith he, "Light burthen's heavy, if far borne":
Quoth I, "The main lost, cast the bye away";
"You have spun a fair thread," he replies in scorn.
   And having thus a while each other thwarted,
   Fools as we met, so fools again we parted.

Since there's no help, come let us kiss and part.
Nay, I have done, you get no more of me,
And I am glad, yea, glad with all my heart,
That thus so cleanly I myself can free;
Shake hands for ever, cancel all our vows,
And when we meet at any time again,

Idea

Be it not seen in either of our brows
That we one jot of former love retain;
Now at the last gasp of Love's latest breath,
When, his pulse failing, Passion speechless lies,
When Faith is kneeling by his bed of death,
And Innocence is closing up his eyes,
    Now if thou wouldst, when all have given him over,
    From death to life thou might'st him yet recover.

ODES

TO THE NEW YEAR

Rich statue, double-fac'd,
With marble temples grac'd,
    To raise thy godhead higher;
In flames where altars shining,
Before thy priests divining,
    Do odorous fumes expire;

Great Janus, I thy pleasure,
With all the Thespian treasure,
    Do seriously pursue;
To the pass'd year returning,
As though the old adjourning,
    Yet bringing in the new.

Thy ancient vigils yearly
I have observed clearly,
    Thy feasts yet smoking be;
Since all thy store abroad is,
Give something to my goddess,
    As hath been us'd by thee.

To the New Year

Give her th' Eoan brightness,
Wing'd with that subtle lightness,
    That doth transpierce the air;
The roses of the morning
The rising heav'n adorning,
    To mesh with flames of hair;

Those ceaseless sounds, above all,
Made by those orbs that move all,
    And ever swelling there,
Wrap'd up in numbers flowing,
Them actually bestowing,
    For jewels at her ear.

O rapture great and holy,
Do thou transport me wholly,
    So well her form to vary;
That I aloft may bear her,
Whereas I will insphere her
    In regions high and starry.

And in my choice composures
The soft and easy closures
    So amorously shall meet;
That every lively ceasure
Shall tread a perfect measure,
    Set on so equal feet.

That spray to fame so fertile,
The lover-crowning myrtle,
    In wreaths of mixed boughs,
Within whose shades are dwelling
Those beauties most excelling,
    Inthron'd upon her brows.

To the New Year

Those parallels so even,
Drawn on the face of heaven,
    That curious art supposes
Direct those gems, whose clearness
Far off amaze by nearness;
    Each globe such fire encloses.

Her bosom full of blisses,
By nature made for kisses,
    So pure and wond'rous clear,
Whereas a thousand Graces
Behold their lovely faces,
    As they are bathing there.

O, thou self-little blindness,
The kindness of unkindness,
    Yet one of those divine,—
Thy brands to me were liever
Thy fascia, and thy quiver,
    And thou this quill of mine.

This heart so freshly bleeding,
Upon its own self feeding,
    Whose wounds still dropping be;
O Love, thy self confounding:
Her coldness so abounding,
    And yet such heat in me.

Yet if I be inspired,
I'll leave thee so admired
    To all that shall succeed,
That were they more than many,
'Mongst all there is not any
    That Time so oft shall read.

To the New Year

Nor adamant engraved,
That hath been choiceliest saved,
   Idea's name outwears ;
So large a dower as this is,
The greatest often misses,
   The diadem that bears.

TO HIS VALENTINE

Muse bid the morn awake,
   Sad winter now declines,
Each bird doth choose a make,
   This day's Saint Valentine's;
For that good bishop's sake
     Get up, and let us see,
     What beauty it shall be
   That fortune us assigns.

But lo, in happy hour,
   The place wherein she lies,
In yonder climbing tow'r,
   Gilt by the glitt'ring rise;
O Jove! that in a show'r,
     As once that thund'rer did,
     When he in drops lay hid,
   That I could her surprise!

Her canopy I'll draw,
   With spangled plumes bedight,
No mortal ever saw
   So ravishing a sight;
That it the gods might awe,
     And powerfully transpierce
     The globy universe,
   Out-shooting ev'ry light.

To his Valentine

My lips I'll softly lay
  Upon her heavenly cheek,
Dyed like the dawning day,
  As polish'd ivory sleek:
And in her ear I'll say:
    O, thou bright morning star,
    Tis I that come so far,
  My Valentine to seek.

Each little bird, this tide,
  Doth choose her loved pheer,
Which constantly abide
  In wedlock all the year,
As nature is their guide:
    So may we two be true
    This year nor change for new,
  As turtles coupled were.

The sparrow, swan, the dove,
  Tho' Venus' birds they be,
Yet are they not for love
  So absolute as we:
For reason us doth move;
    They but by billing woo:
    Then try what we can do,
  To whom each sense is free.

Which we have more than they,
  By livelier organs sway'd,
Our appetite each way
  More by our sense obey'd:
Our passions to display
    This season us doth fit;
    Then let us follow it,
  As nature us doth lead.

To his Valentine

One kiss in two let's break,
    Confounded with the touch;
But half words let us speak,
    Our lips employ'd so much,
Until we both grow weak;
        With sweetness of thy breath,
        O smother me to death;
Long let our joys be such.

Let's laugh at them that choose
    Their Valentines by lot;
To wear their names that use,
    Whom idly they have got:
Such poor choice *we* refuse;
        Saint Valentine befriend,
        We thus this morn may spend,
Else, Muse, awake her not.

THE HEART

If thus we needs must go,
What shall our one heart do,
This one made of our two?

Madam, two hearts we brake
And from them both did take
The best, one heart to make.

Half this is of your heart,
Mine in the other part,
Join'd by our equal art.

Were it cemented, or sewn,
By shreds or pieces known,
We each might find our own.

But 'tis dissolved, and fix'd,
And with such cunning mix'd,
No diff'rence that betwixt.

But how shall we agree,
By whom it kept shall be,
Whether by you, or me?

It cannot two breasts fill,
One must be heartless still,
Until the other will.

The Heart

It came to me to-day,
When I will'd it to say,
With whether it would stay?

It told me: In your breast,
Where it might hope to rest:
For if it were my guest,

For certainty it knew,
That I would still anew
Be sending it to you.

Never, I think had two
Such work, so much to do,
A unity to woo.

Yours was so cold and chaste
Whilst mine with zeal did waste,
Like fire with water plac'd.

How did my heart intreat,
How pant, how did it beat,
Till it could give your's heat!

Till to that temper brought,
Through our perfection wrought,
That blessing either's thought,

In such a height it lies,
From this base world's dull eyes,
That heaven it not envies.

All that this earth can show,
Our heart shall not once know,
For it too vile and low.

TO MY WORTHY FRIEND
MASTER JOHN SAVAGE
OF THE INNER TEMPLE

Upon this sinful earth
If man can happy be,
And higher than his birth,
Friend, take him thus from me.

Whom promise not deceives
That he the breach should rue,
Nor constant reason leaves
Opinion to pursue.

To raise his mean estate
That soothes no wanton's sin;
Doth that preferment hate
That virtue doth not win.

Nor bravery doth admire,
Nor doth more love profess
To that he doth desire
Than that he doth possess.

Loose humour nor to please
That neither spares nor spends,
But by discretion weighs
What is to needful ends.

To him, deserving not,
Not yielding, nor doth hold
What is not his, doing what
He ought, not what he could.

Whom the base tyrants' will
So much could never awe,
As him for good or ill
From honesty to draw.

Whose constancy doth rise
'Bove undeserved spite,
Whose valour's to despise
That most doth him delight.

That early leave doth take
Of th' world, though to his pain,
For virtue's only sake,
And not till need constrain.

No man can be so free,
Though in imperial seat,
Nor eminent as he
That deemeth nothing great.

THE CRIER

Good folk, for gold or hire,
But help me to a crier;
For my poor heart is run astray
After two eyes, that pass'd this way.
  O yes, O yes, O yes,
   If there be any man,
   In town or country, can
   Bring me my heart again,
   I'll please him for his pain;
And by these marks I will you show,
That only I this heart do owe.
  It is a wounded heart,
Wherein yet sticks the dart,
Ev'ry piece sore hurt throughout it,
Faith and troth writ round about it:
It was a tame heart, and a dear,
  And never us'd to roam;
But having got this haunt, I fear
  'Twill hardly stay at home.
For God's sake, walking by the way,
  If you my heart do see,
Either impound it for a stray,
  Or send it back to me.

TO HIS COY LOVE

A Canzonet

I PRAY thee, leave, love me no more,
    Call home the heart you gave me,
I but in vain that saint adore,
    That can, but will not save me:
These poor half kisses kill me quite;
    Was ever man thus served?
Amidst an ocean of delight,
    For pleasure to be starved.

Shew me no more those snowy breasts
    With azure riverets branched,
Where whilst mine eye with plenty feasts,
    Yet is my thirst not stanched.
O Tantalus, thy pains ne'er tell,
    By me thou art prevented;
'Tis nothing to be plagu'd in hell,
    But thus in heaven tormented.

Clip me no more in those dear arms,
    Nor thy life's comfort call me;
O, these are but too powerful charms,
    And do but more enthrall me.
But see how patient I am grown,
    In all this coil about thee;
Come, nice thing, let thy heart alone;
    I cannot live without thee.

TO HIS RIVAL

Her lov'd I most,
By thee that's lost,
Though she were won with leisure;
She was my gain,
But to my pain
Thou spoil'st me of my treasure.

The ship full fraught
With gold, far sought,
Though ne'er so wisely helmed,
May suffer wrack
In sailing back
By tempest overwhelmed.

But she, good sir,
Did not prefer
You, for that I was ranging;
But for that she
Found faith in me,
And she lov'd to be changing.

Therefore boast not
Your happy lot,
Be silent now you have her;
The time I knew
She slighted you,
When I was in her favour.

To his Rival

None stands so fast
But may be cast
By fortune, and disgraced :
Once did I wear
Her garter there
Where you her glove have placed.

I had the vow
That thou hast now
And glances to discover
Her love to me,
And she to thee
Reads but old lessons over.

She hath no smile
That can beguile,
But as my thought I know it ;
Yea, to a hair,
Both when and where
And how she will bestow it.

What now is thine
Was only mine,
And first to me was given ;
Thou laugh'st at me,
I laugh at thee,
And thus we two are even.

But I'll not mourn,
But stay my turn,
The wind may come about, sir,
And once again
May bring me in
And help to bear you out, sir.

BALLAD OF AGINCOURT

FAIR stood the wind for France,
When we our sails advance,
Nor now to prove our chance
    Longer will tarry;
But putting to the main
At Kaux, the mouth of Seine,
With all his martial train
    Landed King Harry.

And taking many a fort
Furnish'd in warlike sort,
Marcheth towards Agincourt
    In happy hour;
Skirmishing day by day
With those that stopp'd his way
Where the French Gen'ral lay
    With all his power.

Which in his height of pride
King Henry to deride,
His ransom to provide
    To the King sending;
Which he neglects the while
As from a nation vile,
Yet with an angry smile
    Their fall portending.

And turning to his men
Quoth our brave Henry then:
"Though they to one be ten,
    Be not amazed:
Yet have we well begun,
Battles so bravely won
Have ever to the sun
    By fame been raised.

"And for myself (quoth he)
This my full rest shall be,
England ne'er mourn for me
    Nor more esteem me:
Victor I will remain
Or on this earth lie slain,
Never shall she sustain
    Loss to redeem me.

"Poitiers and Cressy tell,
When most their pride did swell,
Under our swords they fell:
    No less our skill is
Than when our grandsire great,
Claiming the regal seat,
By many a warlike feat
    Lopp'd the French Lilies."

The Duke of York so dread
The eager vaward led;
With the main Henry sped
    Among'st his henchmen;
Exeter had the rear,
A braver man not there,—
O Lord, how hot they were
    On the false Frenchmen!

Ballad of Agincourt

They now to fight are gone:
Armour on armour shone,
Drum now to drum did groan,—
    To hear was wonder.
That with the cries they make
The very earth did shake;
Trumpet to trumpet spake,
    Thunder to thunder.

Well it thine age became,
O noble Erpingham,
Which did'st the signal aim
    To our hid forces;
When from a meadow by,
Like a storm suddenly,
The English archery
    Stuck the French horses,

With Spanish yew so strong,
Arrows a cloth-yard long,
That like to serpents stung
    Piercing the weather;
None from his fellow starts,
But playing manly parts,
And like true English hearts,
    Stuck close together.

When down their bows they threw
And forth their bilboes drew
And on the French they flew,
    Not one was tardy;
Arms were from shoulders sent,
Scalps to the teeth were rent,
Down the French peasants went
    Our men were hardy.

Ballad of Agincourt

This while our noble King,
His broad-sword brandishing,
Down the French host did ding,
    As to o'erwhelm it;
And many a deep wound lent,
His arms with blood besprent,
And many a cruel dent
    Bruised his helmet.

Gloster, that Duke so good,
Next of the Royal blood,
For famous England stood
    With his brave brother;
Clarence, in steel so bright,
Though but a maiden knight,
Yet in that furious fight
    Scarce such another.

Warwick in blood did wade,
Oxford the foe invade,
And cruel slaughter made
    Still as they ran up:
Suffolk his axe did ply,
Beaumont and Willoughby
Bare them right doughtily,
    Ferrers and Fanhope.

Upon Saint Crispin's day
Fought was this noble fray
Which fame did not delay
    To England to carry:
O when shall English men
With such acts fill a pen,
Or England breed again
    Such a King Harry!

TO THE VIRGINIAN VOYAGE

You brave heroic minds,
Worthy your country's name,
   That honour still pursue;
   Go and subdue,
Whilst loit'ring hinds
Lurk here at home with shame.

Britons, you stay too long;
Quickly aboard bestow you,
   And with a merry gale
   Swell your stretch'd sail,
With vows as strong
As the winds that blow you.

Your course securely steer,
West and by south forth keep;
   Rocks, lee-shores, nor shoals,
   When Eolus scowls,
You need not fear;
So absolute the deep.

And cheerfully at sea
Success you still entice
   To get the pearl and gold,
   And ours to hold
Virginia,
Earth's only Paradise.

To the Virginian Voyage

Where nature hath in store
Fowl, venison, and fish,
   And the fruitful'st soil,
   Without your toil,
Three harvests more,
All greater than your wish.

And the ambitious vine
Crowns with his purple mass
   The cedar reaching high
   To kiss the sky,
The cypress, pine,
And useful sassafras.

To whom the golden age
Still nature's laws doth give,
   No other cares attend
   But them to defend
From winter's rage,
That long there doth not live.

When as the luscious smell
Of that delicious land,
   Above the seas that flows,
   The clear wind throws
Your hearts to swell
Approaching the dear strand;

In kenning of the shore
(Thanks to God first given)
   O you, the happiest men,
   Be frolic then;
Let cannons roar,
Frighting the wide heaven.

And in regions far,
Such heroes bring ye forth,
    As those from whom we came;
    And plant our name
Under that star
Not known unto our North.

And as there plenty grows
Of Laurel everywhere,
    Apollo's sacred tree,
    You it may see,
A poet's brows
To crown, that may sing there.

Thy voyages attend
Industrious Hackluit,
    Whose reading shall inflame
    Men to seek fame,
And much commend
To after-times thy wit.

AN ODE WRITTEN IN THE PEAK

This while we are abroad,
   Shall we not touch our lyre?
Shall we not sing an ode?
   Shall that holy fire,
In us that strongly glow'd,
   In this cold air expire?

Long since the summer laid
   Her lusty brav'ry down,
The autumn half is way'd,
   And Boreas 'gins to frown,
Since now I did behold
   Great Brute's first builded town.

Though in the utmost Peak
   A while we do remain,
Amongst the mountains bleak
   Exposed to sleet and rain,
No sport our hours shall break,
   To exercise our vein.

What though bright Phœbus' beams
   Refresh the southern ground,
And though the princely Thames
   With beauteous nymphs abound,
And by old Camber's streams
   Be many wonders found;

An Ode Written in the Peak

Yet many rivers clear
   Here glide in silver swathes;
And what of all most dear,
   Buxton's delicious baths,
Strong ale and noble cheer,
   To assuage breem winter's scathes.

Those grim and horrid caves,
   Whose looks affright the day,
Wherein nice nature saves
   What she would not bewray,
Our better leisure craves,
   And doth invite our lay.

In places far or near,
   Or famous or obscure,
Where wholesome is the air,
   Or where the most impure,
All times and everywhere,
   The muse is still in ure.

From POLY-OLBION

MILFORD HAVEN

You goodly sister floods, how happy is your state!
Or should I more commend your features or your
 fate,
That Milford, which this isle her greatest port doth
 call,
Before your equal floods is lotted to your fall?
Where was sail ever seen, or wind hath ever blown,
Whence Pembroke yet hath heard of haven like her
 own?
She bids Dungleddy dare Iberia's proudest road
And chargeth her to send her challenges abroad
Along the coast of France, to prove if any be
Her Milford that dare match: so absolute is she.
So highly Milford is in every mouth renowned,
No haven hath aught good in her that is not found.
Whereas the swelling surge, that with his foamy
 head
The gentler-looking land with fury menaced,
With his encountering wave no longer there con-
 tends;
But sitting mildly down like perfect ancient friends,
Unmoved of any wind which way soe'er it blow
And rather seem to smile than knit an angry brow.
The ships with shattered ribs scarce creeping from
 the seas,

Milford Haven

On her sleek bosom ride with such deliberate ease,
As all her passed storms she holds but mean and base
So she may reach at length this most delightful place,
By nature with proud cliffs environed about.
(SONG V.)

GUY OF WARWICK

Thus, whilst in crowds they throng,
Led by the king himself the champion comes along;
A man well strook in years, in homely palmer's gray
And in his hand his staff, his reverend steps to stay,
Holding a comely pace, which at his passing by
In every censuring tongue, as every serious eye,
Compassion mixed with fear, distrust and courage bred.
 Then Colebrond for the Danes came forth in ireful red;
Before him, from the camp, an ensign first displayed
Amidst a guard of gleaves: then sumptuously arrayed
Were twenty gallant youths that to the warlike sound
Of Danish brazen drums, with many a lofty bound,
Came with their country's march, as they to Mars should dance.
Thus forward to the fight both champions them advance:
And each without respect doth resolutely choose
The weapon that he brought, nor doth his foe's refuse:
The Dane prepares his axe, that ponderous was to feel,
Whose squares were laid with plates, and riveted with steel,

And armed down along with pikes, whose hardened
    points,
Forced with the weapon's weight, had power to tear
    the joints
Of cuirass or of mail, or whatsoe'er they took:
Which caused him at the knight disdainfully to look.
   When our stout palmer soon, unknown for
       valiant Guy,
The cord from his straight loins doth presently
    untie,
Puts off his palmer's weed unto his truss, which bore
The stains of ancient arms, but showed it had before
Been costly cloth of gold; and off his hood he threw:
Out of his hermit's staff his two-hand sword he drew
(The unsuspected sheath which long to it had been)
Which till that instant time the people had not seen:
A sword so often tried.   Then to himself quoth he:
"Arms, let me crave your aid, to set my country free,
And never shall my heart your help again require,
But only to my God to lift you up in prayer."
Here Colebrond forward made, and soon the
    Christian knight
Encounters him again with equal power and spite:
  .   .   .   .   .
Where strength still answered strength, on courage
    courage grew.
Look how two lions fierce, both hungry, both
    pursue
One sweet and self-same prey, at one another fly,
And with their armed paws engrappled dreadfully,
The thunder of their rage and boisterous struggling
    make
The neighbouring forests round affrightedly to
    quake:

Their sad encounter such.   The mighty Colebrond
        struck
A cruel blow at Guy : which though he finely broke
Yet with the weapon's weight his ancient hilt it
        split,
And, thereby lessened much, the champion lightly
        hit
Upon the reverend brow : immediately from whence
The blood dropt softly down, as if the wound had
        sense
Of their much inward woe that it with grief should
        see.
    The Danes, a deadly blow supposing it to be,
Sent such an echoing shout that rent the troubled
        air.
The English at the noise waxed all so wan with
        fear
As though they lost the blood their aged champion
        shed.
Yet were not these so pale but the other were as
        red :
As though the blood that fell upon their cheeks
        had staid.
    Here Guy, his better spirits recalling to his aid,
Came fresh upon his foe, when mighty Colebrond
        makes
Another desperate stroke ; which Guy of Warwick
        takes
Undauntedly aloft ; and followed with a blow
Upon his shorter ribs, that the excessive flow
Streamed up unto his hilts : the wound so gaped
        withal
As though it meant to say, Behold your champion's
        fall

By this proud palmer's hand. Such claps again
    and cries
The joyful English gave as cleft the very skies.
Which coming on along from these that were with-
    out,
When those within the town received this cheerful
    shout
They answered then with like ; as those their joy
    that knew.
    Then with such eager blows each other they
        pursue,
As every offer made should threaten imminent
    death :
Until, through heat and toil both hardly drawing
    breath,
They desperately do close. Look how two boars
    being set
Together side to side their threatening tusks do
    whet,
And with their gnashing teeth their angry foam
    do bite,
Whilst still they shouldering seek each other where
    to smite ;
Thus stood those ireful Knights ; till flying back
    at length
The palmer, of the two the first recovering strength,
Upon the left arm lent great Colebrond such a
    wound,
That whilst his weapon's point fell well near to the
    ground,
And slowly he it raised, the valiant Guy again
Sent through his cloven scalp his blade into his
    brain.   (SONG XII.)

AN ELEGY

TO MY MOST DEARLY LOVED FRIEND,

HENRY REYNOLDS, Esquire

Of Poets and Poesie

My dearly loved friend, how oft have we
In winter evenings, meaning to be free,
To some well-chosen place used to retire,
And there, with moderate meat and wine and fire,
Have passed the hours contentedly with chat,
Now talked of this, and then discoursed of that,
Spoke our own verses 'twixt ourselves; if not,
Other men's lines, which we by chance had got,
Or some stage pieces famous long before,
Of which your happy memory had store;
And I remember you much pleased were
Of those who lived long ago to hear,
As well as of those of these latter times
Who have enriched our language with their rimes,
And in succession how still up they grew,—
Which is the subject that I now pursue.
For from my cradle, you must know that I
Was still inclined to noble poesy,
And when that once Pueriles I had read,
And newly had my Cato construéd,
In my small self I greatly marvelled then,
Amongst all other, what strange kind of men

These poets were; and, pleased with the name,
To my mild tutor merrily I came,
(For I was then a proper goodly page,
Much like a pigmy, scarce ten years of age)
Clasping my slender arms about his thigh,
"O, my dear master! cannot you," quoth I,
"Make me a poet? Do it if you can,
And you shall see I'll quickly be a man."
Who me thus answered, smiling, "Boy," quoth he,
"If you'll not play the wag, but I may see
You ply your learning, I will shortly read
Some poets to you." Phœbus be my speed,
To 't hard went I, when shortly he began,
And first read to me honest Mantuan,
Then Virgil's Eclogùes; being entered thus,
Methought I straight had mounted Pegasus,
And in his full career could make him stop
And bound upon Parnassus bi-clift top.
I scorned your ballad then, though it were done
And had for finis William Elderton.
But soft, in sporting with this childish jest,
I from my subject have too long digrest,
Then to the matter that we took in hand:
Jove and Apollo for the Muses stand!
    That noble Chaucer in those former times,
The first enriched our English with his rimes,
And was the first of ours that ever brake
Into the Muses' treasure, and first spake
In weighty numbers, delving in the mine
Of perfect knowledge, which he could refine
And coin for current, and as much as then
The English language could express to men
He made it do, and by his wondrous skill
Gave us much light from his abundant quill.

And honest Gower, who in respect of him
Had only sipped at Aganippe's brim,
And though in years this last was him before,
Yet fell he far short of the other's store.
    When after those, four ages very near,
They with the Muses which conversèd were
That princely Surrey, early in the time
Of the Eighth Henry, who was then the prime
Of England's noble youth; with him there came
Wyat, with reverence whom we still do name
Amongst our poets; Brian had a share
With the two former, which accounted are
That time's best makers, and the authors were
Of those small poems which the title bear
Of songs and sonnets, wherein oft they hit
On many dainty passages of wit.
    Gascoigne and Churchyard after them again,
In the beginning of Eliza's reign,
Accounted were great meterers many a day,
But not inspirèd with brave fire; had they
Lived but a little longer, they had seen
Their works before them to have buried been.
    Grave, moral Spenser after these came on,
Than whom I am persuaded there was none,
Since the blind bard his Iliads up did make,
Fitter a task like that to undertake;
To set down boldly, bravely to invent,
In all high knowledge surely excellent.
    The noble Sidney with this last arose,
That heroë for numbers and for prose,
That throughly paced our language, as to show
The plenteous English hand in hand might go
With Greek and Latin, and did first reduce
Our tongue from Lyly's writing then in use;

An Elegy

Talking of stones, stars, plants, of fishes, flies,
Playing with words and idle similes;
As the English apes and very zanies be
Of everything that they do hear and see,
So imitating his ridiculous tricks,
They spake and writ all like mere lunatics.
    Then Warner, though his lines were not so trimmed,
Nor yet his poem so exactly limned
And neatly jointed but the critic may
Easily reprove him, yet thus let me say
For my old friend, some passages there be
In him, which I protest have taken me
With almost wonder, so fine, clear and new,
As yet they have been equalléd by few.
    Neat Marlowe, bathéd in the Thespian springs,
Had in him those brave translunary things
That the first poets had, his raptures were
All air and fire, which made his verses clear;
For that fine madness still he did retain
Which rightly should possess a poet's brain.
    And surely Nash, though he a proser were,
A branch of laurel yet deserves to bear;
Sharply satiric was he, and that way
He went, since that his being to this day,
Few have attempted; and I surely think
Those words shall hardly be set down with ink
Shall scorch and blast so as his could, where he
Would inflict vengeance; and be it said of thee,
Shakespeare, thou hadst as smooth a comic vein,
Fitting the sock, and in thy natural brain
As strong conception and as clear a rage,
As any one that trafficked with the stage.

An Elegy

Amongst these Samuel Daniel, whom if I
May speak of, but to censure do deny,
Only have heard some wise men him rehearse
To be too much historian in verse;
His rimes were smooth, his metres well did close,
But yet his manner better fitted prose.
Next these, learned Jonson in this list I bring,
Who had drunk deep of the Pierian spring,
Whose knowledge did him worthily prefer,
And long was lord here of the theatre;
Who in opinion made our learn'dst to stick
Whether in poems rightly dramatic
Strong Seneca or Plautus, he or they,
Should bear the buskin or the sock away.
Others again here lived in my days,
That have of us deserved no less praise
For their translations, than the daintiest wit
That on Parnassus thinks he high'st doth sit,
And for a chair may 'mongst the Muses call,
As the most curious maker of them all;
As reverend Chapman, who hath brought to us
Musæus, Homer, and Hesiodus
Out of the Greek; and by his skill hath reared
Them to that height, and to our tongue endeared,
That were those poets at this day alive,
To see their books thus with us to survive,
They would think, having neglected them so long,
They had been written in the English tongue.
And Silvester who from the French more weak
Made Bartas of his six days' labour speak
In natural English, who, had he there stayed
He had done well, and never had bewrayed
His own invention to have been so poor,
Who still wrote less in striving to write more.

An Elegy

    Then dainty Sandys, that hath to English done
Smooth sliding Ovid, and hath made him run
With so much sweetness and unusual grace,
As though the neatness of the English pace
Should tell the jetting Latin that it came
But slowly after, as though stiff and lame.
    So Scotland sent us hither for our own
That man, whose name I ever would have known
To stand by mine, that most ingenious knight,
My Alexander, to whom in his right
I want extremely, yet in speaking thus
I do but show the love that was 'twixt us,
And not his numbers, which were brave and high,
So like his mind was his clear poesie;
And my dear Drummond, to whom much I owe
For his much love, and proud I was to know
His poesy; for which two worthy men,
I Menstry still shall love, and Hawthornden.
Then the two Beaumonts and my Browne arose,
My dear companions, whom I freely chose
My bosom friends; and in their several ways
Rightly born poets, and in these last days
Men of much note, and no less nobler parts,
Such as have freely told to me their hearts,
As I have mine to them. But if you shall
Say in your knowledge that these be not all
Have writ in numbers, be informed that I
Only myself to these few men do tie,
Whose works oft printed, set on every post,
To public censure subject have been most.
For such whose poems, be they ne'er so rare,
In private chambers that encloistered are,
And by transcription daintily must go;
As though the world unworthy were to know

Their rich composures, let those men that keep
These wondrous relics in their judgment deep,
And cry them up so, let such pieces be
Spoke of by those that shall come after me,
I pass not for them ; nor do mean to run
In quest of these that them applause have won
Upon our stages in these latter days,
That are so many ; let them have their bays
That do deserve it ; let those wits that haunt
Those public circuits, let them freely chaunt
Their fine composures and their praise pursue ;
And so, my dear friend, for this time adieu.

NYMPHIDIA

The Court of Fairy

OLD Chaucer doth of Topas tell,
Mad Rabelais of Pantagruel,
A later third of Dowsabel,
    With such poor trifles playing;
Others the like have laboured at,
Some of this thing and some of that,
And many of they know not what,
    But that they must be saying.

Another sort there be, that will
Be talking of the Fairies still,
Nor never can they have their fill,
    As they were wedded to them;
No tales of them their thirst can slake,
So much delight therein they take,
And some strange thing they fain would make,
    Knew they the way to do them.

Then since no Muse hath been so bold,
Or of the later, or the old,
Those elvish secrets to unfold,
    Which lie from others' reading;
My active Muse to light shall bring
The Court of that proud Fairy King,
And tell there of the revelling.
    Jove prosper my proceeding!

And thou, Nymphidia, gentle Fay,
Which, meeting me upon the way,
These secrets didst to me bewray,
    Which now I am in telling;
My pretty, light, fantastic maid,
I here invoke thee to my aid,
That I may speak what thou hast said,
    In numbers smoothly swelling.

This palace standeth in the air,
By necromancy placéd there,
That it no tempests needs to fear,
    Which way soe'er it blow it.
And somewhat southward tow'rd the noon,
Whence lies a way up to the moon,
And thence the Fairy can as soon
    Pass to the earth below it.

The walls of spiders' legs are made
Well mortiséd and finely laid;
He was the master of his trade
    It curiously that builded;
The windows of the eyes of cats,
And for the roof, instead of slats,
Is covered with the skins of bats,
    With moonshine that are gilded.

Hence Oberon him sport to make,
Their rest when weary mortals take,
And none but only fairies wake,
    Descendeth for his pleasure;
And Mab, his merry Queen, by night
Bestrides young folks that lie upright,
(In elder times, the mare that hight,)
    Which plagues them out of measure.

Nymphidia

Hence shadows, seeming idle shapes,
Of little frisking elves and apes
To earth do make their wanton scapes,
    As hope of pastime hastes them;
Which maids think on the hearth they see
When fires well-near consumèd be,
There dancing hays by two and three,
    Just as their fancy casts them.

These make our girls their sluttery rue,
By pinching them both black and blue,
And put a penny in their shoe
    The house for cleanly sweeping;
And in their courses make that round
In meadows and in marshes found,
Of them so called the Fairy Ground,
    Of which they have the keeping.

These when a child haps to be got
Which after proves an idiot
When folk perceive it thriveth not,
    The fault therein to smother,
Some silly, doting, brainless calf
That understands things by the half,
Say that the Fairy left this oaf
    And took away the other.

But listen, and I shall you tell
A chance in Faëry that befell,
Which certainly may please some well
    In love and arms delighting,
Of Oberon that jealous grew
Of one of his own Fairy crew,
Too well, he feared, his Queen that knew,
    His love but ill requiting.

Pigwiggin was this Fairy Knight,
One wondrous gracious in the sight
Of fair Queen Mab, which day and night
    He amorously observéd;
Which made King Oberon suspect
His service took too good effect,
His sauciness and often checkt,
    And could have wished him starvéd.

Pigwiggin gladly would commend
Some token to Queen Mab to send,
If sea or land could ought him lend
    Were worthy of her wearing;
At length this lover doth devise
A bracelet made of emmet's eyes,
A thing he thought that she would prize,
    No whit her state impairing.

And to the Queen a letter writes,
Which he most curiously indites,
Conjuring her by all the rites
    Of love, she would be pleaséd
To meet him, her true servant, where
They might, without suspect or fear,
Themselves to one another clear
    And have their poor hearts easéd.

"At midnight the appointed hour;
And for the Queen a fitting bower,"
Quoth he, "is that fair cowslip flower
    On Hipcut hill that bloweth:
In all your train there's not a fay
That ever went to gather may
But she hath made it, in her way;
    The tallest there that groweth."

Nymphidia

When by Tom Thumb, a Fairy Page,
He sent it, and doth him engage
By promise of a mighty wage
    It secretly to carry;
Which done, the Queen her maids doth call,
And bids them to be ready all:
She would go see her summer hall,
    She could no longer tarry.

Her chariot ready straight is made
Each thing therein is fitting laid,
That she by nothing might be stayed,
    For nought must her be letting;
Four nimble gnats the horses were,
Their harnesses of gossamer,
Fly Cranion her charioteer
    Upon the coach-box getting.

Her chariot of a snail's fine shell,
Which for the colours did excel,
The fair Queen Mab becoming well,
    So lively was the limning;
The seat the soft wool of the bee,
The cover, gallantly to see,
The wing of a pied butterflee;
    I trow 'twas simple trimming.

The wheels composed of crickets' bones,
And daintily made for the nonce,
For fear of rattling on the stones
    With thistle-down they shod it;
For all her maidens much did fear
If Oberon had chanc'd to hear
That Mab his Queen should have been there,
    He would not have abode it.

She mounts her chariot with a trice,
Nor would she stay, for no advice,
Until her maids that were so nice
    To wait on her were fitted;
But ran herself away alone,
Which when they heard, there was not one
But hasted after to be gone,
    As she had been diswitted.

Hop and Mop and Drop so clear,
Pip and Trip and Skip that were
To Mab, their sovereign, ever dear,
    Her special maids of honour;
Fib and Tib and Pink and Pin,
Tick and Quick and Jill and Jin,
Tit and Nit and Wap and Win,
    The train that wait upon her.

Upon a grasshopper they got
And, what with amble and with trot,
For hedge nor ditch they spared not,
    But after her they hie them;
A cobweb over them they throw,
To shield the wind if it should blow,
Themselves they wisely could bestow
    Lest any should espy them.

But let us leave Queen Mab awhile,
(Through many a gate, o'er many a stile,
That now had gotten by this wile),
    Her dear Pigwiggin kissing;
And tell how Oberon doth fare,
Who grew as mad as any hare
When he had sought each place with care
    And found his Queen was missing.

By grisly Pluto he doth swear,
He rent his clothes and tore his hair,
And as he runneth here and there
    An acorn cup he greeteth,
Which soon he taketh by the stalk,
About his head he lets it walk,
Nor doth he any creature balk,
    But lays on all he meeteth.

The Tuscan Poet doth advance
The frantic Paladin of France,
And those more ancient do enhance
    Alcides in his fury,
And others Ajax Telamon,
But to this time there hath been none
So Bedlam as our Oberon,
    Of which I dare assure ye.

And first encountering with a Wasp,
He in his arms the fly doth clasp
As though his breath he forth would grasp,
    Him for Pigwiggin taking:
"Where is my wife, thou rogue?" quoth he;
"Pigwiggin, she is come to thee;
Restore her, or thou diest by me!"
    Whereat the poor Wasp quaking

Cries, "Oberon, great Fairy King,
Content thee, I am no such thing:
I am a Wasp, behold my sting!"
    At which the Fairy started;
When soon away the Wasp doth go,
Poor wretch, was never frighted so;
He thought his wings were much too slow,
    O'erjoyed they so were parted.

He next upon a Glow-worm light,
(You must suppose it now was night),
Which, for her hinder part was bright,
    He took to be a devil,
And furiously doth her assail
For carrying fire in her tail ;
He thrashed her rough coat with his flail ;
    The mad King feared no evil.

"Oh!" quoth the Glow-worm, "hold thy hand,
Thou puissant King of Fairy-land !
Thy mighty strokes who may withstand ?
    Hold, or of life despair I ! "
Together then herself doth roll,
And tumbling down into a hole
She seemed as black as any coal ;
    Which vext away the Fairy.

From thence he ran into a hive :
Amongst the bees he letteth drive,
And down their combs begins to rive,
    All likely to have spoiléd,
Which with their wax his face besmeared,
And with their honey daubed his beard :
It would have made a man afeared
    To see how he was moiléd.

A new adventure him betides ;
He met an Ant, which he bestrides,
And post thereon away he rides,
    Which with his haste doth stumble,
And came full over on her snout ;
Her heels so threw the dirt about,
For she by no means could get out,
    But over him doth tumble.

Nymphidia

And being in this piteous case,
And all be-slurréd head and face,
On runs he in this wild-goose chase,
    As here and there he rambles;
Half blind, against a molehole hit,
And for a mountain taking it,
For all he was out of his wit
    Yet to the top he scrambles.

And being gotten to the top,
Yet there himself he could not stop,
But down on the other side doth chop,
    And to the foot came rumbling;
So that the grubs, therein that bred,
Hearing such turmoil overhead,
Thought surely they had all been dead;
    So fearful was the jumbling.

And falling down into a lake,
Which him up to the neck doth take,
His fury somewhat it doth slake;
    He calleth for a ferry;
Where you may some recovery note,
What was his club he made his boat,
And in his oaken cup doth float,
    As safe as in a wherry.

Men talk of the adventures strange
Of Don Quixote, and of their change
Through which he arméd oft did range,
    Of Sancho Pancha's travel;
But should a man tell everything
Done by this frantic Fairy King,
And them in lofty numbers sing,
    It well his wits might gravel.

Scarce set on shore, but therewithal
He meeteth Puck, which most men call
Hobgoblin, and on him doth fall
    With words from frenzy spoken:
"Oh, oh," quoth Hob, "God save thy grace!
Who drest thee in this piteous case?
He thus that spoiled my sovereign's face,
    I would his neck were broken!"

This Puck seems but a dreaming dolt,
Still walking like a ragged colt,
And oft out of a bush doth bolt,
    Of purpose to deceive us;
And leading us makes us to stray,
Long winter's nights, out of the way;
And when we stick in mire and clay,
    Hob doth with laughter leave us.

"Dear Puck," quoth he, "my wife is gone:
As e'er thou lov'st King Oberon,
Let everything but this atone,
    With vengeance and pursue her;
Bring her to me alive or dead,
Or that vile thief, Pigwiggin's head,
That villain hath my Queen misled;
    He to this folly drew her."

Quoth Puck, "My liege, I'll never lin,
But I will thorough thick and thin,
Until at length I bring her in;
    My dearest lord, ne'er doubt it.
Thorough brake, thorough briar,
Thorough muck, thorough mire,
Thorough water, thorough fire;
    And thus goes Puck about it."

Nymphidia

This thing Nymphidia overheard,
That on this mad king had a guard,
Not doubting of a great reward
    For first this business broaching;
And through the air away doth go,
Swift as an arrow from the bow,
To let her sovereign Mab to know
    What peril was approaching.

The Queen bound with Love's powerful'st charm
Sate with Pigwiggin arm in arm;
Her merry maids, that thought no harm,
    About the room were skipping;
A humble-bee, their minstrel, played
Upon his hautboy, every maid
Fit for this revel was arrayed,
    The hornpipe neatly tripping.

In comes Nymphidia, and doth cry,
"My sovereign, for your safety fly,
For there is danger but too nigh;
    I posted to forewarn you:
The King hath sent Hobgoblin out,
To seek you all the fields about,
And of your safety you may doubt,
    If he but once discern you."

When, like an uproar in a town,
Before them everything went down;
Some tore a ruff, and some a gown,
    'Gainst one another justling;
They flew about like chaff i' th' wind;
For haste some left their masks behind;
Some could not stay their gloves to find;
    There never was such bustling.

Forth ran they, by a secret way,
Into a brake that near them lay;
Yet much they doubted there to stay,
    Lest Hob should hap to find them;
He had a sharp and piercing sight,
All one to him the day and night;
And therefore were resolved by flight
    To leave this place behind them.

At length one chanced to find a nut,
In the end of which a hole was cut,
Which lay upon a hazel root,
    There scattered by a squirrel
Which out the kernel gotten had;
When quoth this Fay, "Dear Queen, be glad;
Let Oberon be ne'er so mad,
    I'll set you safe from peril.

"Come all into this nut," quoth she,
"Come closely in; be ruled by me;
Each one may here a chooser be,
    For room ye need not wrastle:
Nor need ye be together heaped;"
So one by one therein they crept,
And lying down they soundly slept,
    And safe as in a castle.

Nymphidia, that this while doth watch,
Perceived if Puck the Queen should catch
That he should be her over-match,
    Of which she well bethought her;
Found it must be some powerful charm,
The Queen against him that must arm,
Or surely he would do her harm,
    For throughly he had sought her.

And listening if she aught could hear,
That her might hinder, or might fear;
But finding still the coast was clear;
　　Nor creature had descried her;
Each circumstance and having scanned,
She came thereby to understand,
Puck would be with them out of hand;
　　When to her charms she hied her.

And first her fern-seed doth bestow,
The kernel of the mistletoe;
And here and there as Puck should go,
　　With terror to affright him,
She night-shade strews to work him ill,
Therewith her vervain and her dill,
That hindereth witches of their will,
　　Of purpose to despite him.

Then sprinkles she the juice of rue,
That groweth underneath the yew;
With nine drops of the midnight dew,
　　From lunary distilling:
The molewarp's brain mixed therewithal;
And with the same the pismire's gall:
For she in nothing short would fall,
　　The Fairy was so willing.

Then thrice under a briar doth creep,
Which at both ends was rooted deep,
And over it three times she leap;
　　Her magic much availing:
Then on Proserpina doth call,
And so upon her spell doth fall,
Which here to you repeat I shall,
　　Not in one tittle failing.

"By the croaking of the frog;
By the howling of the dog;
By the crying of the hog
    Against the storm arising;
By the evening curfew bell,
By the doleful dying knell,
O let this my direful spell,
    Hob, hinder thy surprising!

"By the mandrake's dreadful groans;
By the lubrican's sad moans;
By the noise of dead men's bones
    In charnel-houses rattling;
By the hissing of the snake,
The rustling of the fire-drake,
I charge thee thou this place forsake,
    Nor of Queen Mab be prattling!

"By the whirlwind's hollow sound,
By the thunder's dreadful stound,
Yells of spirits underground,
    I charge thee not to fear us;
By the screech-owl's dismal note,
By the black night-raven's throat,
I charge thee, Hob, to tear thy coat
    With thorns, if thou come near us!"

Her spell thus spoke, she stept aside,
And in a chink herself doth hide,
To see thereof what would betide,
    For she doth only mind him:
When presently she Puck espies,
And well she marked his gloating eyes,
How under every leaf he pries,
    In seeking still to find them.

Nymphidia

But once the circle got within,
The charms to work do straight begin,
And he was caught as in a gin;
    For as he thus was busy,
A pain he in his head-piece feels,
Against a stubbéd tree he reels,
And up went poor Hobgoblin's heels;
    Alas! his brain was dizzy!

At length upon his feet he gets,
Hobgoblin fumes, Hobgoblin frets;
And as again he forward sets,
    And through the bushes scrambles,
A stump doth trip him in his pace;
Down comes poor Hob upon his face,
And lamentably tore his case,
    Amongst the briars and brambles.

"A plague upon Queen Mab!" quoth he,
"And all her maids where'er they be:
I think the devil guided me,
    To seek her so provokéd!"
When stumbling at a piece of wood,
He fell into a ditch of mud,
Where to the very chin he stood,
    In danger to be chokéd.

Now worse than e'er he was before,
Poor Puck doth yell, poor Puck doth roar,
That waked Queen Mab, who doubted sore
    Some treason had been wrought her:
Until Nymphidia told the Queen,
What she had done, what she had seen,
Who then had well-near cracked her spleen
    With very extreme laughter.

But leave we Hob to clamber out,
Queen Mab and all her Fairy rout,
And come again to have a bout
    With Oberon yet madding:
And with Pigwiggin now distraught,
Who much was troubled in his thought,
That he so long the Queen had sought,
    And through the fields was gadding.

And as he runs he still doth cry,
"King Oberon, I thee defy,
And dare thee here in arms to try,
    For my dear lady's honour:
For that she is a Queen right good,
In whose defence I'll shed my blood,
And that thou in this jealous mood
    Hast laid this slander on her."

And quickly arms him for the field,
A little cockle-shell his shield,
Which he could very bravely wield:
    Yet could it not be piercéd:
His spear a bent both stiff and strong,
And well near of two inches long:
The pile was of a horse-fly's tongue,
    Whose sharpness nought reverséd.

And puts him on a coat of mail,
Which was of a fish's scale,
That when his foe should him assail,
    No point should be prevailing:
His rapier was a hornet's sting;
It was a very dangerous thing,
For if he chanced to hurt the King,
    It would be long in healing.

Nymphidia

His helmet was a beetle's head,
Most horrible and full of dread,
That able was to strike one dead,
    Yet did it well become him;
And for a plume a horse's hair
Which, being tosséd with the air,
Had force to strike his foe with fear,
    And turn his weapon from him.

Himself he on an earwig set,
Yet scarce he on his back could get,
So oft and high he did curvét,
    Ere he himself could settle:
He made him turn, and stop, and bound,
To gallop and to trot the round,
He scarce could stand on any ground,
    He was so full of mettle.

When soon he met with Tomalin,
One that a valiant knight had been,
And to King Oberon of kin;
    Quoth he, "Thou manly Fairy,
Tell Oberon I come prepared,
Then bid him stand upon his guard;
This hand his baseness shall reward,
    Let him be ne'er so wary.

"Say to him thus, that I defy
His slanders and his infamy,
And as a mortal enemy
    Do publicly proclaim him:
Withal that if I had mine own,
He should not wear the Fairy crown,
But with a vengeance should come down,
    Nor we a king should name him."

This Tomalin could not abide
To hear his sovereign vilified;
But to the Fairy Court him hied,
    (Full furiously he posted,)
With everything Pigwiggin said:
How title to the crown he laid,
And in what arms he was arrayed,
    As how himself he boasted.

'Twixt head and foot, from point to point,
He told the arming of each joint,
In every piece how neat and quaint,
    For Tomalin could do it:
How fair he sat, how sure he rid,
As of the courser he bestrid
How managed, and how well he did;
    The King which listened to it,

Quoth he, "Go, Tomalin, with speed,
Provide me arms, provide my steed,
And everything that I shall need;
    By thee I will be guided;
To straight account call thou thy wit;
See there be wanting not a whit,
In everything see thou me fit,
    Just as my foe's provided."

Soon flew this news through Fairy-land,
Which gave Queen Mab to understand
The combat that was then in hand
    Betwixt those men so mighty:
Which greatly she began to rue,
Perceiving that all Faëry knew
The first occasion from her grew
    Of these affairs so weighty.

Nymphidia

Wherefore attended with her maids,
Through fogs, and mists, and damps she wades,
To Proserpine the Queen of Shades,
    To treat, that it would please her
The cause into her hands to take,
For ancient love and friendship's sake,
And soon thereof an end to make,
    Which of much care would ease her.

A while there let we Mab alone,
And come we to King Oberon,
Who, armed to meet his foe, is gone,
    For proud Pigwiggin crying:
Who sought the Fairy King as fast,
And had so well his journeys cast,
That he arrivéd at the last,
    His puissant foe espying.

Stout Tomalin came with the King,
Tom Thumb doth on Pigwiggin bring
That perfect were in everything
    To single fights belonging:
And therefore they themselves engage
To see them exercise their rage
With fair and comely equipage,
    Not one the other wronging.

So like in arms these champions were,
As they had been a very pair,
So that a man would almost swear
    That either had been either;
Their furious steeds began to neigh,
That they were heard a mighty way;
Their staves upon their rests they lay
    Yet ere they flew together

Their seconds minister an oath,
Which was indifferent to them both,
That on their knightly faith and troth
    No magic them supplied;
And sought them that they had no charms
Wherewith to work each other's harms,
But came with simple open arms
    To have their causes tried.

Together furiously they ran,
That to the ground came horse and man,
The blood out of their helmets span,
    So sharp were their encounters;
And though they to the earth were thrown,
Yet quickly they regained their own,
Such nimbleness was never shown,
    They were two gallant mounters.

When in a second course again,
They forward came with might and main,
Yet which had better of the twain,
    The seconds could not judge yet;
Their shields were into pieces cleft,
Their helmets from their heads were reft,
And to defend them nothing left,
    These champions would not budge yet.

Away from them their staves they threw,
Their cruel swords they quickly drew,
And freshly they the fight renew,
    They every stroke redoubled;
Which made Proserpina take heed,
And make to them the greater speed,
For fear lest they too much should bleed,
    Which wondrously her troubled.

Nymphidia

When to the infernal Styx she goes,
She takes the fogs from thence that rose,
And in a bag doth them enclose,
    When well she had them blended.
She hies her then to Lethe spring,
A bottle and thereof doth bring,
Wherewith she meant to work the thing
    Which only she intended.

Now Proserpine with Mab is gone
Unto the place where Oberon
And proud Pigwiggin, one to one,
    Both to be slain were likely:
And there themselves they closely hide,
Because they would not be espied;
For Proserpine meant to decide
    The matter very quickly.

And suddenly unties the poke,
Which out of it sent such a smoke,
As ready was them all to choke,
    So grievous was the pother;
So that the knights each other lost,
And stood as still as any post;
Tom Thumb nor Tomalin could boast
    Themselves of any other.

But when the mist 'gan somewhat cease,
Proserpina commandeth peace;
And that a while they should release
    Each other of their peril:
"Which here," quoth she, "I do proclaim
To all in dreadful Pluto's name,
That as ye will eschew his blame,
    You let me hear the quarrel:

"But here yourselves you must engage,
Somewhat to cool your spleenish rage;
Your grievous thirst and to assuage
    That first you drink this liquor,
Which shall your understanding clear,
As plainly shall to you appear;
Those things from me that you shall hear
    Conceiving much the quicker."

This Lethe water, you must know,
The memory destroyeth so,
That of our weal, or of our woe,
    Is all remembrance blotted;
Of it nor can you ever think;
For they no sooner took this drink,
But nought into their brains could sink
    Of what had them besotted.

King Oberon forgotten had
That he for jealousy ran mad,
But of his Queen was wondrous glad,
    And asked how they came thither:
Pigwiggin likewise doth forget
That he Queen Mab had ever met,
Or that they were so hard beset,
    When they were found together.

Nor neither of them both had thought
That e'er they had each other sought,
Much less that they a combat fought,
    But such a dream were loathing.
Tom Thumb had got a little sup,
And Tomalin scarce kissed the cup,
Yet had their brains so sure locked up,
    That they remembered nothing.

Queen Mab and her light maids, the while,
Amongst themselves do closely smile,
To see the King caught with this wile,
    With one another jesting:
And to the Fairy Court they went
With mickle joy and merriment,
Which thing was done with good intent,
    And thus I left them feasting.

THE SHEPHERD'S SIRENA

Dorilus in sorrows deep,
Autumn waxing old and chill,
As he sat his flocks to keep
Underneath an easy hill,
Chanc'd to cast his eye aside
On those fields where he had seen
Bright Sirena, nature's pride,
Sporting on the pleasant green;
To whose walks the shepherds oft
Came, her godlike foot to find,
And in places that were soft
Kissed the print there left behind:
Where the path which she had trod
Hath thereby more glory gain'd
Than in Heav'n that milky road
Which with nectar Hebe stain'd.
But bleak winter's boist'rous blasts
Now their fading pleasures chid,
And so fill'd them with his wastes
That from sight her steps were hid.
Silly shepherd sad the while
For his sweet Sirena gone,
All his pleasures in exile,
Laid on the cold earth alone;
Whilst his gamesome cut-tailed cur
With his mirthless master plays

The Shepherd's Sirena

Striving him with sport to stir
As in his more youthful days.
Dorilus his dog doth chide,
Lays his well-tun'd bagpipe by,
And his sheep-hook casts aside;
There (quoth he) together lie.
When a letter forth he took,
Which to him Sirena writ,
With a deadly down-cast look,
And thus fell to reading it.
    Dorilus, my dear (quoth she),
Kind companion of my woe,
Though we thus divided be,
Death cannot divorce us so.
Thou whose bosom hath been still
Th' only closet of my care,
And in all my good and ill
Ever had thy equal share;
Might I win thee from thy fold,
Thou should'st come to visit me,
But the winter is so cold
That I fear to hazard thee.
The wild waters are waxed high,
So they are both deaf and dumb,
Lov'd they thee so well as I
They would ebb when thou should'st come;
Then my cot with light should shine,
Purer than the vestal fire;
Nothing here but should be thine
That thy heart can well desire:
Where at large we will relate
From what cause our friendship grew,
And in that the varying fate
Since we first each other knew;

Of my heavy passed plight,
As of many a future fear,
Which except the silent night
None but only thou shalt hear.
My sad heart it shall relieve
When my thoughts I shall disclose,
For thou can'st not choose but grieve
When I shall recount my woes:
There is nothing to that friend
To whose close uncrannied breast
We our secret thoughts may send,
And there safely let it rest.
And thy faithful counsel may
My distressed case assist;
Sad affliction else may sway
Me a woman as it list.
Hither I would have thee haste,
Yet would gladly have thee stay,
When those dangers I forecast
That may meet thee by the way
Do as thou shalt think it best;
Let thy knowledge be thy guide;
Live thou in my constant breast
Whatsoever shall betide.
    He her letter having read
Puts it in his scrip again,
Looking like a man half-dead,
By her kindness strangely slain;
And as one who inly knew
Her distressed present state,
And to her had still been true,
Thus doth with himself debate.
    I will not thy face admire,
Admirable though it be,

The Shepherd's Sirena

Nor thine eyes whose subtile fire
So much wonder win in me;
But my marvel shall be now
(And of long it hath been so)
Of all womankind that thou
Wert ordain'd to taste of woe.
To a beauty so divine,
Paradise in little done,
O that fortune should assign
Ought but what thou well mightst shun.
But my counsels such must be
(Though as yet I them conceal)
By their deadly wound in me
They thy hurt must only heal.
Could I give what thou do'st crave,
To that pass thy state is grown
I thereby thy life may save
But am sure to lose mine own.
To that joy thou dost conceive,
Through my heart the way doth lie;
Which in two for thee must cleave,
Lest that thou shouldst go awry.
Thus my death must be a toy
Which my pensive breast must cover;
Thy beloved to enjoy
Must be taught thee by thy lover.
Hard the choice I have to choose;
To myself if friend I be
I must my Sirena lose;
If not so, she loseth me.
    Thus whilst he doth cast about
What therein were best to do,
Nor could yet resolve the doubt
Whether he should stay or go;

In those fields not far away
There was many a frolic swain
In fresh russets day by day
That kept revels on the plain:
Nimble Tom, sirnam'd the Tup,
For his pipe without a peer,
And could tickle Trenchmore up
As 'twould joy your heart to hear;
Ralph, as much renown'd for skill,
That the Tabor touch'd so well;
For his Gittern little Gill,
That all other did excel;
Rock and Rollo every way
Who still led the rustic ging,
And could troll a roundelay
That would make the fields to ring;
Colin on his shawm so clear
Many a high-pitcht note that had
And could make the echos near
Shout as they were waxen mad.
Many a lusty swain beside,
That for nought but pleasure car'd,
Having Dorilus espi'd
And with him knew how it far'd,
Thought from him they would remove
This strong melancholy fit,
Or so, should it not behove,
Quite to put him out of's wit;
Having learnt a song which he
Sometime to Sirena sent,
Full of jollity and glee,
When the nymph liv'd near to Trent;
They behind him softly got,
Lying on the earth along,

And when he suspected not
Thus the jovial shepherds sung.
   Near to the silver Trent
     Sirena dwelleth,
She to whom nature lent
   all that excelleth;
By which the Muses late
   and the neat Graces
Have for their greater state
   taken their places:
Twisting an Anadem
   wherewith to crown her,
As it belong'd to them
   most to renown her,
     Chorus.—On thy bank
         In a rank
           Let thy swans sing her,
         And with their music
           along let them bring her.

Tagus and Pactolus
   are to thee debter,
Nor for their gold to us,
   are they the better:
Henceforth of all the rest
   be thou the river,
Which as the daintiest
   puts them down ever;
For as my precious one
   o'er thee doth travel
She to pearl paragon
   turneth thy gravel.
      Chorus.—On thy bank
         In a rank

        Let thy swans sing her,
        And with their music
           along let them bring her.

Our mournful Philomel
  that rarest tuner,
Henceforth in Apëril
  shall wake the sooner.
And to her shall complain
  from the thick cover,
Redoubling every strain
  over and over;
For when my love too long
  her chamber keepeth,
As though it suffered wrong
  the morning weepeth.
      Chorus.—On thy bank
        In a rank
        Let thy swans sing her,
        And with their music
           along let them bring her.

Oft have I seen the sun,
  to do her honour,
Fix himself, at his noon,
  to look upon her,
And hath gilt every grove
  every hill near her
With his flames from above
  striving to cheer her;
And when she from his sight
  hath herself turned,
He as it had been night
  in clouds hath mourned.

The Shepherd's Sirena

> *Chorus.*—On thy bank
>   In a rank
>   Let thy swans sing her,
>   ·And with their music
>   along let them bring her.

The verdant meads are seen,
  when she doth view them,
In fresh and gallant green
  straight to renew them;
And every little grass
  broad itself spreadeth,
Proud that this bonny lass
  upon it treadeth;
Nor flower is so sweet
  in this large cincture,
But it upon her feet
  leaveth some tincture.
> *Chorus.*—On thy bank
>   In a rank
>   Let thy swans sing her,
>   And with their music
>   along let them bring her.

The fishes in the flood,
  when she doth angle
For the hook strive a good
  them to entangle.
And leaping on the land
  from the clear water
Their scales upon the sand
  lavishly scatter;
Therewith to pave the mould
  whereon she passes

The Shepherd's Sirena

So herself to behold
   as in her glasses.
     Chorus.—On thy bank
       In a rank
         Let thy swans sing her,
       And with their music
         along let them bring her.

When she looks out by night
   the stars stand gazing,
Like comets to our sight
   fearfully blazing,
As wondering at her eyes
   with their much brightness,
Which so amaze the skies,
   dimming their lightness;
The raging tempests are calm,
   when she speaketh,
Such most delightsome balm
   from her lips breaketh.
     Chorus.—On thy bank,
       In a rank
         Let thy swans sing her,
       And with their music
         along let them bring her.

In all our Brittany
   there's not a fairer,
Nor can you fit any
   should you compare her;
Angels her eye-lids keep,
   all hearts surprising,
Which look, whilst she doth sleep,
   like the sun's rising:

The Shepherd's Sirena

She alone of her kind
  knoweth true measure,
And her unmatched mind
  is heavens treasure.
    Chorus.—On thy bank
      In a rank
      Let thy swans sing her,
      And with their music
        along let them bring her.

Fair Dove and Darwen clear,
  boast ye your beauties,
To Trent your mistress here
  yet pay your duties;
My love was higher born,
  towards the full fountains,
Yet she doth moorland scorn
  and the Peak mountains;
Nor would she none should dream
  where she abideth,
Humble as is the stream
  which by her slideth.
    Chorus.—On thy bank
      In a rank
      Let the swans sing her,
      And with their music
        along let them bring her.

Yet my poor rustic muse
  nothing can move her,
Nor the means I can use
  though her true lover:
Many a long winter's night
  have I wak'd for her,

The Shepherd's Sirena

  Yet this my piteous plight
   nothing can stir her:
  All thy sands, silver Trent,
   down to the Humber,
  The sighs that I have spent
   never can number.
    Chorus.—On thy bank
      In a rank
     Let thy swans sing her,
     And with their music
      along let them bring her.

Taken with this sudden song,
Least for mirth when he doth look,
His sad heart more deeply stung
Than the former care he took;
At their laughter and amaz'd,
For a while he sat aghast
But a little having gaz'd
Thus he then bespoke at last.
  Is this time for mirth (quoth he)
To a man with grief opprest,
Sinful wretches as you be,
May the sorrows in my breast
Light upon you one by one,
And as now you mock my woe,
When your mirth is turn'd to moan
May your like then serve you so.
  When one swain among the rest
Thus him merrily bespake:
Get thee up, thou arrant beast;
Fits this season love to make?
Take thy sheep-hook in thy hand,
Clap thy cur and set him on;

The Shepherd's Sirena

For our fields 'tis time to stand,
Or they quickly will be gone.
Roguish swineherds that repine
At our flocks, like beastly clowns,
Swear that they will bring their swine
And will root up all our downs.
They their holly whips have brac'd,
And tough hazel goads have got;
Soundly they your sides will baste
If their courage fail them not.
Of their purpose if they speed
Then your bagpipes you may burn;
It is neither drone nor reed,
Shepherd, that will serve your turn.
Angry Olcon sets them on
And against us part doth take,
Ever since he was out-gone
Off'ring rhymes with us to make.
Yet, if so our sheep-hooks hold,
Dearly shall our downs be bought;
For it never shall be told
We our sheep-walks sold for naught.
And we here have got us dogs
Best of all the Western breed,
Which, though whelps, shall lug their hogs
Till they make their ears to bleed:
Therefore, shepherd, come away.
Whenas Dorilus arose
Whistles cut-tail from his play,
And along with them he goes.

From THE MUSES' ELYSIUM

DESCRIPTION OF ELYSIUM

A PARADISE on earth is found
Though far from vulgar sight,
Which with those pleasures doth abound
That it Elysium hight.

Where in delights that never fade
The muses lulled be,
And sit at pleasure in the shade
Of many a stately tree,

Which no rough tempest makes to reel,
Nor their straight bodies bows;
Their lofty tops do never feel
The weight of winter's snows.

In groves that evermore are green,
No falling leaf is there,
But Philomel (of birds the queen)
In music spends the year.

The Merle upon her myrtle perch
There to the Mavis sings,
Who from the top of some curled birch
Those notes redoubled rings.

Description of Elysium

There daisies damask every place,
Nor once their beauties lose,
That when proud Phœbus hides his face,
Themselves they scorn to close.

The pansy and the violet here,
As seeming to descend
Both from one root, a very pair,
For sweetness yet contend.

And pointing to a pink to tell
Which bears it, it is loath
To judge it, but replies for smell
That it excels them both.

Wherewith displeased they hang their heads,
So angry soon they grow,
And from their odoriferous beds
Their sweets at it they throw.

The winter here a summer is,
No waste is made by time,
Nor doth the autumn ever miss
The blossoms of the prime.

The flower that July forth doth bring
In April here is seen;
The primrose that puts on the spring
In July decks each green.

The sweets for sovereignty contend,
And so abundant be,
That to the very earth they lend
And bark of every tree.

Description of Elysium

Rills rising out of every bank
In wild meanders strain,
And playing many a wanton prank
Upon the speckled plain,

In gambols and lascivious gyres
Their time they still bestow,
Nor to their fountains none retires
Nor on their course will go:

Those brooks with lilies bravely decked
So proud and wanton made,
That they their courses quite neglect
And seem as though they stayed,

Fair Flora in her state to view,
Which through those lilies looks,
Or as those lilies lean'd to shew
Their beauties to the brooks;

That Phœbus in his lofty race
Oft lays aside his beams,
And comes to cool his glowing face
In these delicious streams.

Oft spreading vines climb up the cleeves
Whose ripened clusters there
Their liquid purple drop, which drives
A vintage through the year:

Those cleeves whose craggy sides are clad
With trees of sundry suits,
Which make continual summer glad,
Even bending with their fruits;

Description of Elysium

Some ripening, ready some to fall,
Some blossom'd, some to bloom,
Like gorgeous hangings on the wall
Of some rich, princely room.

Pomegranates, lemons, citrons so
Their laded branches bow,
Their leaves in number that outgo
Nor roomth will them allow.

There in perpetual summer's shade
Apollo's Prophets sit
Among the flowers that never fade
But flourish like their wit;

To whom the nymphs upon their lyres
Tune many a curious lay,
And with their most melodious choirs
Make short the longest day.

The thrice three virgins heavenly clear
Their trembling timbrels sound
Whilst the three comely graces there
Dance many a dainty round.

Decay nor age there nothing knows;
There is continual youth:
As time on plant or creatures grows,
So still their strength renewth.

The Poets' paradise this is,
To which but few can come;
The Muses' only bower of bliss,
Their dear Elysium.

Description of Elysium

Here happy souls (their blessed bowers
Free from the rude resort
Of beastly people) spend the hours
In harmless mirth and sport.

Then on to the Elysian plains
Apollo doth invite you,
Where he provides with pastoral strains
In Nymphals to delight you.

THE SECOND NYMPHAL

Lalus, Cleon and Lirope

The Muse new courtship doth devise
By nature's strange varieties
Whose rarities she here relates,
And gives you pastoral delicates.

Lalus, a jolly, youthful lad,
With Cleon, no less crown'd
With virtues, both their beings had
On the Elisian ground ;
Both having parts so excellent
That it a question was
Which should be the most eminent
Or did in ought surpass.
This Cleon was a mountaineer
And of the wilder kind,
And from his birth had many a year
Been nursed up by a hind ;
And, as the sequel well did show,
It very well might be,
For never hart nor hare nor roe
Were half so swift as he.
But Lalus in the vale was bred
Amongst the sheep and neat,
And by those nymphs there choicely fed
With honey, milk and wheat:

Of stature goodly, fair of speech,
And of behaviour mild
Like those there in the valley rich
That bred him of a child.
Of falconry they had the skill
Their hawks to feed and fly,
No better hunters ere clomb hill
Nor holloa'd to a cry:
In dingles deep and mountains hoar
Oft with the bearded spear
They combated the tusky boar,
And slew the angry bear.
In music they were wondrous quaint;
Fine airs they could devise;
They very curiously could paint
And neatly poetise:
That wagers many time were laid
On questions that arose
Which song the witty Lalus made,
Which Cleon should compose.
The stately steed they manag'd well;
Of fence the art they knew;
For dancing they did all excel
The girls that to them drew.
To throw the sledge, to pitch the bar,
To wrestle and to run,
They all the youth excelled so far
That still the prize they won.
These sprightly gallants lov'd a lass,
Called Lirope the bright;
In the whole world there scarcely was
So delicate a wight.
There was no beauty so divine
That ever nymph did grace,

The Second Nymphal

But it beyond itself did shine
In her more heavenly face.
What form she pleased each thing would take
That ere she did behold;
Of pebbles she could diamonds make,
Gross iron turn to gold.
Such power there with her presence came
Stern tempests she allayed;
The cruel tiger she could tame,
The raging torrents staid.
She chid, she cherished, she gave life,
Again she made to die;
She raised a war, appeased a strife
With turning of her eye.
Some said a god did her beget,
But much deceived were they;
Her Father was a Rivulet
Her Mother was a Fay.
Her lineaments, so fine that were,
She from the fairy took;
Her beauties and complexion clear
By nature from the brook.
These rivals waiting for the hour
(The weather calm and fair)
When as she us'd to leave her bower
To take the pleasant air,
Accosting her, their compliment
To her their goddess done,
By gifts they tempt her to consent:
When Lalus thus begun.

Lalus. Sweet Lirope, I have a lamb,
Newly weaned from the dam,
Of the right kind, it is notted,
Naturally with purple spotted:

Into laughter it will put you
To see how prettily 'twill butt you,
When on sporting it is set
It will beat you a curvet,
And at every nimble bound
Turn itself above the ground.
When 'tis hungry it will bleat
From your hand to have its meat
And when it hath fully fed
It will fetch jumps above your head,
As innocently to express
Its silly sheepish thankfulness;
When you bid it, it will play,
Be it either night or day.
This, Lirope, I have for thee
So thou alone wilt live with me.

 Cleon. From him, O turn thine ear away
And hear me, my lov'd Lirope,
I have a kid as white as milk,
His skin as soft as Naples silk;
His horns in length are wondrous even
And curiously by nature writhen;
It is of th' Arcadian kind;
There's not the like 'twixt either Inde.
If you walk 'twill walk you by,
If you sit down it down will lie;
It with gesture will you woo
And counterfeit those things you do;
O'er each hillock it will vault
And nimbly do the somersault;
Upon the hinder legs 'twill go
And follow you a furlong so;
And if by chance a tune you rote
'Twill foot it finely to your note.

The Second Nymphal

Seek the world and you may miss
To find out such a thing as this.
This, my love, I have for thee
So thou'lt leave him and go with me.
   Lirope. Believe me, youths, your gifts are rare,
And you offer wondrous fair;
Lalus for lamb, Cleon for kid,—
'Tis hard to judge which most doth bid.
And have you two such things in store
And I ne'er knew of them before?
Well, yet I dare a wager lay
That Brag my little dog shall play
As dainty tricks when I shall bid
As Lalus' lamb or Cleon's kid.
But t'may fall out that I may need them:
Till when ye may do well to feed them.
Your goat and mutton pretty be,
But, youths, these are no baits for me.
Alas, good men, in vain ye woo;
'Tis not your lamb nor kid will do.
   Lalus. I have two sparrows white as snow,
Whose pretty eyes like sparks do show:
In her bosom Venus hatched them
Where her little Cupid watched them,
Till they two fledge their nests forsook,
Themselves and to the fields betook;
Where by chance a fowler caught them,
Of whom I full dearly bought them.
They'll fetch you conserve from the hip
And lay it softly on your lip;
Through their nibbling bills they'll chirrup
And fluttering feed you with the sirrup;
And, if thence you put them by
They to your white neck will fly;

And, if you expulse them there,
They'll hang upon your braided hair.
You so long shall see them prattle
Till at length they'll fall to battle,
And when they have fought their fill
You will smile to see them bill.
These birds my Lirope's shall be
So thou'lt leave him and go with me.
 Cleon. His sparrows are not worth a rush;
I'll find as good in every bush.
Of doves I have a dainty pair
Which, when you please to take the air,
About your head shall gently hover
Your clear brow from the sun to cover,
And with their nimble wings shall fan you
That neither cold nor heat shall tan you;
And like umbrellas with their feathers
Shield you in all sorts of weathers;
They be most dainty coloured things,
They have damask backs and chequered wings;
Their necks more various colours show
Than there be mixed in the bow.
Venus saw the lesser dove
And therewith was far in love,
Offering for't her golden ball
For her son to play withal.
These my Lirope's shall be,
So she'll leave him and go with me.
 Lirope. Then for sparrows and for doves
I am fitted 'twixt my loves.
But, Lalus, I take no delight
In sparrows, for they'll scratch and bite
'Twixt Venus' breasts if they have lain
I much fear they'll infect mine.

The Second Nymphal

Cleon, your doves are very dainty,
Tame pigeons else you know are plenty:
These may win some of your marrows,
I am not caught with doves nor sparrows.
I thank ye kindly for your cost,
Yet your labour is but lost.
    Lalus. With full-leav'd lilies I will stick
Thy braided hair all o'er so thick
That from it a light shall throw
Like the sun's upon the snow.
Thy mantle shall be violet-leaves,
With the fin'st the silkworm weaves
As finely woven, whose rich smell
The air about thee so shall swell
That it shall have no power to move.
A ruff of pinks thy robe above,
About thy neck so neatly set
That art it cannot counterfeit,
Which still shall look so fresh and new
As if upon their roots they grew.
And for thy head I'll have a tire
Of netting, made of strawberry wire,
And in each knot, that doth compose
A mesh, shall stick a half-blown rose,
Red, damask, white; in order set
About the sides shall run a fret
Of primroses, the tire throughout
With thrift and daisies fringed about.
All this, fair nymph, I'll do for thee
So thou'lt leave him and go with me.
    Cleon. These be but weeds and trash he brings
I'll give thee solid, costly things.
His will wither and be gone
Before thou well canst put them on;

With coral I will have thee crowned,
Whose branches, intricately wound,
Shall girt thy temples every way;
And on the top of every spray
Shall stick a pearl orient and great,
Which so the wandring birds shall cheat
That some shall stoop to look for cherries
As other for tralucent berries,
And wondring caught ere they be ware
In the curl'd trammels of thy hair.
And for thy neck a crystal chain,
Whose links, shap'd like to drops of rain,
Upon thy panting breast depending
Shall seem as they were still descending,
And, as thy breath doth come and go,
So seeming still to ebb and flow:
With amber bracelets cut like bees,
Whose strange transparency who sees,
With silk small as the spider's twist
Doubled so oft about thy wrist,
Would surely think alive they were,
From lilies gathering honey there.
Thy buskins ivory, carv'd like shells
Of scollop, which, as little bells
Made hollow, with the air shall chime
And to thy steps shall keep the time.
Leave Lalus, Lirope, for me,
And these shall thy rich dowry be.

 Lirope. Lalus for flowers, Cleon for gems!
For garlands and for diadems
I shall be sped. Why, this is brave:
What nymph can choicer presents have?
With dressing, braiding, frowncing, flowering,
All your jewels on me pouring,

In this bravery being dressed
To the ground I shall be pressed;
That I doubt the nymphs will fear me
Nor will venture to come near me.
Never Lady of the May
To this hour was half so gay,
All in flowers, all so sweet
From the crown, beneath the feet.
Amber, coral, ivory, pearl!
If this cannot win a girl
There's nothing can, and this ye woo me.
Give me your hands and trust ye to me
(Yet to tell ye I am loth)
That I'll have neither of you both.
    Lalus. When thou shalt please to stem the flood
(As thou art of the wat'ry brood)
I'll have twelve swans more white than snow
Yok'd for the purpose, two and two,
To draw thy barge wrought of fine reed
So well that it nought else shall need.
The traces by which they shall hale
Thy barge shall be the winding trail
Of woodbind whose brave tassel'd flowers
(The sweetness of the woodnymphs' bowers)
Shall be the trappings to adorn
The swans by which thy barge is borne.
Of flowered flags I'll rob the bank,
Of water cans and king-cups rank,
To be the covering of thy boat;
And, on the stream as thou dost float,
The Naiades that haunt the deep
Themselves about thy barge shall keep,
Recording most delightful lays
By sea-gods written in thy praise.

And in what place thou hapst to land,
There the gentle, silvery sand
Shall soften, curled with the air
As sensible of thy repair.
This, my dear love, I'll do for thee
So thou'lt leave him and go with me.
 Cleon. Tush, nymph, his swans will prove but geese,
His barge drink water like a fleece.
A boat is base : I'll thee provide
A chariot wherein Jove may ride :
In which when bravely thou art borne
Thou shalt look like the glorious morn
Ushering the sun, and such a one
As to this day was never none ;
Of the rarest Indian gums
More precious than your balsamums
Which I by art have made so hard
That they with tools may well be carv'd
To make a coach of ; which shall be
Materials of this one for thee ;
And of thy chariot each small piece
Shall inlaid be with amber-gris
And gilded with the yellow ore
Produc'd from Tagus' wealthy shore :
In which along the pleasant lawn
With twelve white stags thou shalt be drawn,
Whose branched palms of a stately height
With several nosegays shall be dight,
And as thou rid'st thy coach about
For thy strong guard shall run a rout
Of estriges, whose curled plumes
Sens'd with thy chariot's rich perfumes
The scent into the air shall throw ;

Whose naked thighs shall grace the show,
Whilst the woodnymphs and those bred
Upon the mountains, o'er thy head
Shall bear a canopy of flowers
Tinseled with drops of April showers
Which shall make more glorious shows
Than spangles or your silver oes.
This, bright nymph, I'll do for thee,
So thou'lt leave him and go with me.

   Lirope. Vie and revie, like chapmen profer'd
Would't be received what you have offer'd:
Ye greater honour cannot do me,
If not building altars to me.
Both by water and by land,
Barge and chariot at command;
Swans upon the stream to tow me,
Stags upon the land to draw me!
In all this pomp should I be seen,
What a poor thing were a queen.
All delights in such excess
As but ye, who can express?
Thus mounted should the nymphs me see,
All the troop would follow me,
Thinking by this state that I
Would assume a deity.
There be some in love have been,
And I may commit that sin;
And if e'er I be in love,
With one of you I fear 'twill prove.
But with which I cannot tell:
So, my gallant youths, farewell.

THE SIXTH NYMPHAL

SILVIUS, HALCIUS, MELANTHUS

A woodman, fisher, and a swain
This nymphal through with mirth maintain,
Whose pleadings so the Nymphs do please,
That presently they gave them bays.

Clear had the day been from the dawn,
All chequered was the sky,
Thin clouds like scarfs of cobweb lawn
Veiled heaven's most glorious eye.
The wind had no more strength than this,
That leisurely it blew,
To make one leaf the next to kiss
That closely by it grew.
The rills that on the pebbles played
Might now be heard at will;
This world they only music made,
Else everything was still.
The flowers like brave embroidered girls
Looked as they much desired
To see whose head with orient pearls
Most curiously was tired;
And to itself the subtle air
Such sovereignty assumes
That it receiv'd too large a share
From nature's rich perfumes.

The Sixth Nymphal

When the Elysian youth were met
That were of most account,
And to disport themselves were set
Upon an easy mount:
Near which of stately fir and pine
There grew abundant store,
The tree that weepeth turpentine,
And shady sycamore:
Amongst this merry youthful train
A forester they had,
A fisher, and a shepherd's swain,
A lively country lad:
Betwixt which three a question grew
Who should the worthiest be,
Which violently they pursue
Nor stickled would they be;
That it the company doth please,
This civil strife to stay,
Freely to hear what each of these
For his brave self could say:
When first this forester (of all)
That Silvius had to name,
To whom the lot being cast doth fall,
Doth thus begin the game.

Silvius. For my profession then and for the life
    I lead
All others to excel, thus for myself I plead!
I am the prince of sports, the forest is my fee,
He's not upon the earth for pleasure lives like me.
The morn no sooner puts her rosy mantle on
But from my quiet lodge I instantly am gone,
When the melodious birds from every bush and
    briar
Of the wild spacious wastes make a continual choir;

The motlied meadows then, new varnisht with the
    sun,
Shoot up their spicy sweets upon the winds that
    run
In easily ambling gales and softly seem to pace
That it the longer might their lusciousness embrace.
I am clad in youthful green, I other colours scorn;
My silken baldrick bears my bugle or my horn,
Which setting to my lips I wind so loud and
    shrill
As makes the echos shout from every neighbour-
    ing hill.
My dog-hook at my belt, to which my lyam's tied,
My sheaf of arrows by, my woodknife at my side,
My crossbow in my hand, my gaffle on my rack
To bend it when I please, or, if I list, to slack;
My hound then in my lyam, I by the woodman's
    art
Forecast where I may lodge the goodly high-palm'd
    hart,
To view the grazing herds, so sundry times I use,
Where by the loftiest head I know my deer to
    choose;
And to unherd him then I gallop o'er the ground
Upon my well-breath'd nag to cheer my earning
    hound.
Sometime I pitch my toils the deer alive to take,
Sometime I like the cry the deep-mouth'd kennel
    make,
Then underneath my horse I stalk my game to
    strike
And with a single dog to hunt him hurt I like.
The Silvians are to me true subjects, I their king:
The stately hart his hind doth to my presence bring,

The buck his loved doe, the roe his tripping mate,
Before me to my bower whereas I sit in state.
The Dryads, Hamadryads, the Satyrs and the
    Fawns
Oft play at hide and seek before me on the lawns;
The frisking fairy oft when horned Cynthia shines
Before me as I walk dance wanton Matachynes;
The numerous feathered flocks that the wild forests
    haunt
Their silvan songs to me in cheerful ditties chant;
The shades like ample shields defend me from the
    sun
Through which me to refresh the gentle rivulets
    run:
No little bubbling brook from any spring that falls
But on the pebbles plays me pretty madrigals.
I' th' morn I climb the hills, where wholesome
    winds do blow;
At noontide to the vales and shady groves below;
T'wards evening I again the crystal floods frequent:
In pleasure thus my life continually is spent.
As princes and great lords have palaces, so I
Have in the forests here my hall and gallery,
The tall and stately woods, which underneath are
    plain;
The groves my gardens are, the heath and downs
    again
My wide and spacious walks: then say all what
    ye can,
The forester is still your only gallant man.
   He of his speech scarce made an end
   But him they load with praise,
   The nymphs most highly him commend
   And vow to give him bays:

He's now cried up of every one,
And who but only he?
The forester's the man alone,
The worthiest of the three:
When some than the other far more staid,
Will'd them a while to pause
For there was more yet to be said
That might deserve applause:
When Halcius his turn next plies,
And silence having won,
"Room for the fisher man!" he cries,
And thus his plea begun.

Halcius. No, forester, it so must not be borne away,
But hear what for himself the fisher first can say.
The crystal current streams continually I keep
Where every pearl-pav'd ford and every blue-eyed deep
With me familiar are; when in my boat being set
My oar I take in hand, my angle and my net
About me; like a prince myself in state I steer
Now up, now down the stream, now am I here, now there,
The pilot and the fraught myself; and at my ease
Can land me when I list or in what place I please.
The silver-scaled shoals about me in the streams,
As thick as ye discern the atoms in the beams,
Near to the shady bank where slender sallows grow
And willows their shag'd tops down t'wards the waters bow
I shove in with my boat to shield me from the heat,
Where choosing from my bag some prov'd especial bait,

The goodly well grown trout I with my angle strike,
And with my bearded wire I take the ravenous
 pike,
Of whom when I have hold he seldom breaks
 away
Though at my line's full length so long I let him
 play
Till by my hand I find he well-near wearied be,
When softly by degrees I draw him up to me.
The lusty salmon too I oft with angling take,
Which me above the rest most lordly sport doth make,
Who feeling he is caught such frisks and bounds
 doth fetch
And by his very strength my line so far doth stretch
As draws my floating cork down to the very ground
And wresting of my rod doth make my boat turn
 round.
I never idle am; sometime I bait my wheels
With which by night I take the dainty silver eels;
And with my draught-net then I sweep the stream-
 ing flood,
And to my trammel next and cast-net from the mud
I beat the scaly brood; no hour I idly spend,
But wearied with my work I bring the day to end.
The Naiades and Nymphs that in the rivers keep,
Which take into their care the store of every deep,
Amongst the flowery flags, the bulrushes and reed
That of the spawn have charge (abundantly to breed)
Well mounted upon swans their naked bodies lend
To my discerning eye and on my boat attend,
And dance upon the waves before me (for my sake)
To th' music the soft wind upon the reeds doth make;
And for my pleasure more the rougher gods of seas
From Neptune's Court send in the blue Neriades,

Which from his bracky realm upon the billows ride
And bear the rivers back with every streaming tide;
Those billows 'gainst my boat borne with delight-
 ful gales
Oft seeming as I row to tell me pretty tales,
Whilst ropes of liquid pearl still load my labouring
 oars
As stretch'd upon the stream they strike me to the
 shores;
The silent meadows seem delighted with my lays
As sitting in my boat I sing my lass's praise.
Then let them that like the forester up cry;
Your noble fisher is your only man, say I.
 This speech of Halcius turn'd the tide
 And brought it so about
 That all upon the fisher cried
 That he would bear it out;
 Him, for the speech he made, to clap
 Who lent him not a hand,
 And said 'twould be the waters' hap
 Quite to put down the land?
 This while Melanthus silent sits
 (For so the shepherd hight)
 And having heard these dainty wits
 Each pleading for his right;
 To hear them honour'd in this wise
 His patience doth provoke,
 When "For a shepherd room," he cries,
 And for himself thus spoke.
 Melanthus. Well, fisher, you have done, and
 forester for you
Your tale is neatly told, s'are both, to give you due,
And now my turn comes next; then hear a shepherd
 speak.

The Sixth Nymphal

My watchfulness and care gives day scarce leave to
 break
But to the fields I haste, my folded flock to see;
Where when I find nor wolf nor fox hath injur'd me,
I to my bottle straight and soundly baste my throat,
Which done some country song or roundelay I roat
So merrily, that to the music that I make
I force the lark to sing ere she be well awake.
Then Ball my cut-tailed cur and I begin to play,
He o'er my sheep-hook leaps now th' one, now th'
 other way
Then on his hinder feet he doth himself advance;
I tune, and to my note my lively dog doth dance;
Then whistle in my fist, my fellow swains to call;
Down go our hooks and scrips and we to nine holes
 fall,
At dust-point or at quoits else are we at it hard;
All false and cheating games we shepherds are
 debarred.
Surveying of my sheep, if ewe or wether look
As though it were amiss, or with my cur or crook
I take it, and when once I find what it doth ail
It hardly hath that hurt but that my skill can heal.
And when my careful eye I cast upon my sheep
I sort them in my pens and sorted so I keep:
Those that are big'st of bone I still reserve for breed,
My cullings I put off or for the chapman feed.
When the evening doth approach I to my bagpipe
 take,
And to my grazing flocks such music then I make
That they forbear to feed; then me a king you see,
I playing go before, my subjects follow me;
My bell-wether most brave before the rest doth
 stalk,

The father of the flock, and after him doth walk
My writhen-headed ram with posies crowned in
      pride
Fast to his crooked horns with ribands neatly tied.
And at our shepherds' board that's cut out of the
      ground,
My fellow swains and I together at it round,
With greencheese, clotted cream, with flawns and
      custards stored,
Whig, cider and with whey I domineer a lord.
When shearing time is come I to the river drive
My goodly well-fleec'd flocks (by pleasure thus I
      thrive);
Which being washed at will upon the shearing day
My wool I forth in locks fit for the winder lay,
Which upon lusty heaps into my cot I heave
That in the handling feels as soft as any sleeve;
When every ewe two lambs that yeaned hath that
      year
About her new-shorn neck a chaplet then doth
      wear.
My tarbox and my scrip, my bagpipe at my back,
My sheep-hook in my hand, what can I say I lack?
He that a sceptre swayed, a sheep-hook in his hand
Hath not disdained to have; for shepherds then I
      stand.
Then, forester, and you, my fisher, cease your strife,
I say your shepherd leads your only merry life.
      They had not cried the forester
      And fisher up before
      So much, but now the nymphs prefer
      The shepherd ten times more;
      And all the song goes on his side,
      Their minion him they make,

To him themselves they all apply
And all his party take;
Till some in their discretion cast,
Since first the strife begun
In all that from them there had passed
None absolutely won;
That equal honour they should share,
And their deserts to show
For each a garland they prepare
Which they on them bestow,
Of all the choicest flowers that were,
Which purposely they gather;
With which they crown them, parting there
As they came first together.

NOTES

[Handwritten note: Cf. Drummond "Fl. of Sion". "Nature must yield to Grace." "Too long I followed have fond desire, And too long panted on deluding streams" &c.]

Page 4, l. 2. *Paint on floods till the shore cry to the air.* I do not grasp the poet's imagery. That 'paint' is what Daniel wrote seems certain from what looks like an expansion of the line in Drayton's *Idea*, sonnet 45.

> " Muses which sadly sit about my chair,
> Drown'd in the tears extorted by my lines,
> With heavy sighs while thus I break the air,
> Painting my passions in these sad designs."

Moreover, the *Errata* in 1611 corrects a misprint in this line but says nothing about 'paint.' The word is frequently used simply for 'utter,' and probably is so here, and the meaning may be no more than this, that the poet as he sits by the waterside infects the shore with his passion. *Cf.* Civil War, ii. 129 [ed. 1595]—

> "Nor had I then *at solitary brook*
> Sat framing bloody accents of these times"

[altered in 1602 to 'Nor had my Muse so sad a subject took,' and omitted in 1623]. Whether the 'floods' are caused by the lover's tears, and the shore cries out in fear of being submerged, is more than I can say.

p. 6, l. 16. *arcs of love*, *i.e.* eyebrows.
p. 14, l. 23. *arcs*, *i.e.* triumphal arches.
p. 15, l. 1. *the Roman.* Q. Mucius Scævola.
p. 23, l. 10. *at last.* I have supplied these words to fill out the metre and the sense.
p. 26, l. 6. *smoke.* So 1602. Every edition I have seen subsequent to this, including Grosart's, reads *smoakt*, which gives no sense. Cf. *Epistle to Countess of Cumberland*, p. 34—

> " The all-gniding Providence doth yet
> All disappoint, and mocks this smoke of wit."

p. 30. This passage of the 'Death of Talbot' was a great favourite with Coleridge, especially the stanza beginning, 'Whilst Talbot, whose fresh ardour,' etc. In a letter to Charles Lamb he says: "You must read over these *Civil Wars* again. Gravely sober in all ordinary affairs, and not easily excited by any—yet there is one on which his Blood boils—whenever he speaks of English valour exerted against a foreign Enemy. . . . Thousands even of educated men would become more sensible, fitter to be members of Parliament or ministers, by reading Daniel—and even those few, who *quoad intellectum* only gain refreshment of notions already their own, must become better Englishmen." (Quoted by Morris.)

p. 35, l. 33. *Knowing the heart of man*, etc. This stanza was quoted by Wordsworth in the Fourth Book of the Excursion. In a note he transcribes the four stanzas beginning, 'Nor is he moved with all the thunder-cracks,' as containing "an admirable picture of the state of a wise man's mind in a time of public commotion." 'The whole poem,' he adds, 'is very beautiful.' In a letter to Lady Beaumont he speaks of it as "composed in a strain of meditative morality more dignified and affecting than any thing of the kind I ever read." The modern reader is apt to miss the imagery here. It is a comparison of man to the universe. All the terms, *revolution, aspect, predominate*, etc., are borrowed from the Ptolemaic system of astronomy. In line 2 I have restored the correct reading '*his* world,' which Grosart does not note, from 1602 ed. For the familiar thought of man as the microcosm, *cf.* p. 38, l. 5.

p. 36, l. 11. *dispense with*, come to terms with, a favourite word with Daniel.

p. 37, l. 5. *of*, 1602. Texts usually read *that*, Grosart does not even note the true reading. Probably by the 'gold of leaden minds' Daniel means panegyric.

p. 39, l. 1. Wordsworth borrowed this line for the opening of the 18th sonnet to the river Duddon; but omitted the first two words from his quotation marks.

Notes

p. 46, l. 11. All the editions read 'rest with me;' which both spoils the rhyme and supplies no antithesis to the 'here' two lines below.

p. 49, l. 11. *area.* I take credit for restoring the true reading from the edition of 1611. Every edition since, that I have seen, including Grosart's, reads 'air,' which neither scans nor makes sense.

p. 51. Hymen's Triumph richly deserves a reprint. Coleridge said of it: "Hymen's Triumph exhibits a continued series of first-rate beauties in thought, passion, and imagery; and in language and metre is so faultless, that the style of that poem may, without extravagance, be declared to be imperishable English" (*Literary Remains*, ii. 360).

p. 55. The Ode was first published in Daniel's volume of 1594 at the end of the Sonnets. In the collected volume of 1623 it is printed twice. As Daniel's happiest song, I give it the place of honour at the end of this selection.

p. 57. *Daffadill.* I leave Drayton's spelling of this word, as he uses it for a proper name. Moreover, his spelling is recognised by Skeat.

p. 62, l. 10. *Sest.* Sestos.

p. 63, l. 1. "The Duke of Longaville, which was Prisoner in England, upon the Peace to be concluded between England and France, was delivered; and married the Princess Mary, for Lewes the French King his master."—DRAYTON'S NOTE.

p. 64, l. 13. "The Duke of Suffolk, when the Proclamation came into England of jousts to be holden in France at Paris, he for the Queen's sake, his Mistress, obtained of the King to go thither: with whom went the Marquess Dorset and his four brothers, the Lord Clinton, Sir Edward Nevill, Sir Giles Campbell, Thomas Cheyney, which went all over with the Duke as his assistants."—DRAYTON'S NOTE.

l. 20. *biss*, silk.

p. 65, l. 13. "Francis Valoys, the Dolphin of France, envying the glory that the English men had obtained at the Tilt, brought in an Almain secretly, a man thought almost of incomparable strength, which encountred Charles Brandon at the barriers; but the Duke, grappling with him, so beat him about the head with the pommel of his sword, that the blood came out of the sight of his casque."—DRAYTON'S NOTE.

p. 66, l. 9. "Sir William Brandon, standard-bearer to the Earl of Richmond (after Henry the Seventh) at Bosworth Field, a brave and gallant gentleman, who was slain by Richard there; this was father to this Charles Brandon, Duke of Suffolk."—DRAYTON'S NOTE.

p. 68. *Princes like Suns.* From 'Queen Isabel to Richard II.'

Love's September. From 'Queen Margaret to William de la Poole, Duke of Suffolk.'

l. 12. *breem*, stormy; a word 'taken from Lydgate by Spenser, and echoed by later poets,' Murray, *s.v.*

p. 69. From the Barons' Wars, Book vi., 30-63.

p. 70, l. 12. *sledge*, sledge-hammer.

l. 25. *landscape*, a painter's word for the background of a picture. This is the earliest instance of its use that I remember to have met. It does not come in the first version; of which I give three stanzas here for the sake of comparison:—

"Here cliffy Cynthus, with a thousand birds
 Whose checkered plumes adorn his tufted crown,
 Under whose shadow graze the straggling herds,
 Out of whose top the fresh springs tumbling down
  Duly keep time with their harmonious soun[d];
 The rock so lively done in every part
 As Art had so taught Nature, Nature Art.

"Here falls proud Phaëton, tumbling through the clouds
 The sunny palfreys have their traces broke,
 And setting fire upon the welked shrouds
 Now through the heaven fly gadding from the yoke,
  The Spheres all reeking with a misty smoke,
 Drawn with such life, as some did much desire
 To warm themselves, some frighted with the fire.

"Upon the sundry pictures they devise,
 And from one thing they to another run;
 Now they commend that body, then those eyes,
 How well that bird, how well that flower was done,
  The lively counterfeiting of that sun;
 The colours, the conceits, the shadowings,
 And in that art a thousand sundry things."

p. 73, l. 17. *crankling,* winding.
p. 74, l. 3. *cauples,* horses; from low latin *caballus* (Murray).
p. 76. Drayton first printed sonnets in a book called ' Ideas Mirrour. Amours in Quatorzains' (1594), reprinted by Collier in 1856. These (51 in number) were added to, corrected, and selected from, in various editions, until in the collected poems of 1619 there were 63, including for the first time the famous sonnet, 'Since there's no help,' etc. Mr Elton in his masterly 'Introduction to Drayton' (printed for the Spenser Society) has a very full bibliography, with a special appendix on the Sonnets. He calls attention to two which Drayton did not reprint (the first and eighth of this selection) as being 'of a rare and excellent Spenserian vintage.'
p. 77, l. 14. *too good to be disgraced.* Supply 'they are.'
p. 88. *Odes.* Mr Collier notes that 'the application of the word Ode at this date [1606] was nearly new in our language.' Daniel had employed it in 1592 (see page 55). Drayton writes a preface defending the name, and instancing classical authorities, such as Pindar, Anacreon, and Horace. He calls his own a 'mixed' style of Ode like that of Horace, 'little partaking of the high dialect of Pindar, nor altogether of Anacreon, the arguments being amorous, moral, or what else the Muse pleaseth.' Some of them are in the manner of Skelton. The introductory Ode 'To himself and the harp,' in which he gives a history and defence of the Ode form, concludes thus:

> " Nor is't the Verse doth make,
> That giveth or doth take;
> 'Tis possible to climb,
> To kindle or to slake,
> Although in Skelton's rime."

'All matter and no art' is dangerous doctrine, and the Skeltoniads, though it is certainly possible to climb them with an effort, the modern reader finds intolerably rugged. The smoothest may be quoted here, as a confession of Drayton's poetical faith:

Notes

> "The Muse should be sprightly
> Yet not handling lightly
> Things grave; as much loth
> Things that be slight to clothe
> Curiously; to retain
> The comeliness in mean
> Is true knowledge and wit.
> Nor me forced rage doth fit
> That I thereto should lack
> Tobacco, or the sack,
> Which to the colder brain
> Is the true Hippocrene.
> Nor did I ever care
> For great fools nor great fare :
> Virtue though neglected
> Is not so dejected
> As vilely to descend
> To low baseness, their end.
> Neither each rhyming slave
> Deserves the name to have
> Of poet : so the rabble
> Of fools for the table,
> That have their jests by heart,
> As an actor his part,
> Might assume them chairs
> Amongst the Muse's heirs.
> Parnassus is not clomb
> By every such nome ;
> Up whose steep side who swerves
> It behoves have strong nerves.
> My resolution such,
> How well, and not how much,
> I write : thus do I fare
> Like some few good, that care
> (The evil sort among)
> How well to live, and not how long."

p. 89, l. 1. *Eoan.* Eos is the dawn.

    l. 22. *ceasure, i.e. cæsura,* defined by Sidney as 'the breathing place in the midst of a verse.' The word is used by Spenser (F. Q., II. x. 68).

> 'There abruptly it did end,
> Without full point, or other *ceasure* right.'

p. 90, l. 13. This and the next stanza are an address to Cupid.

    l. 17. *fascia,* fillet.

p. 92, l. 3. *make,* mate.

p. 95, l. 8. *mine in the other part.* Perhaps *in* should be *is.*

p. 103. The original title of this poem is "To my friends the Camber-britons and theyr Harp." In 1619 it

Notes

was altered to "To the Cambro-Britans and their Harpe, his Ballad of Agincourt." In the preface to *both* editions he thus speaks of it: "[I] would at this time also gladly let thee understand what I think above the rest, of the last Ode of this number (or if thou wilt Ballad) in my Book: for both the great master of Italian rymes, Petrarch, and our Chaucer, and other of the upper house of the Muses, have thought their canzons honoured in the title of a Ballad; which for that I labour to meet truly therein with the old English garb, I hope as able to justify as the learned Colin Clout [*i.e.* Spenser] his roundelay."

p. 105, l. 26. *bilboes.* Swords were so called, as coming from Bilboa. Thus both the English weapons, sword and bow, were from Spain.

p. 107. There are many variations in this and the previous poem between the editions of 1606 and 1619. For the most part the later text has been followed.

p. 108, l. 12. *Sassafras.* A laurel formerly much used in medicine.

p. 109, l. 14. *Hackluit*, Rev. Richard, the famous geographer, author of 'The Principall Navigations, Voiages, and Discoveries of the English Nation made by sea or over land to the most remote and farthest distant quarters of the earth, at any time within the compass of these 1500 yeares' (1589, augmented 1590).

p. 111, l. 18. *ure*, use.

p. 118, l. 19. *Pueriles*, *i.e.* 'Sententiæ Pueriles,' a well-known Latin phrase-book.

l. 20. *Cato*, *i.e.* Dionysius Cato, who wrote *Disticha de moribus*, once a famous school-book.

p. 119, l. 20. *William Elderton*, a writer of ballads.

p. 120, l. 11. *Brian*, Sir Francis, the favourite of Henry VIII., called 'Sacred Brian' in the *Heroical Epistles*, wrote in Tottell's Miscellany but without signing his pieces, which are therefore now not distinguishable.

p. 121, l. 15. *Neat Marlowe.* I should conjecture *next*, were it not for the phrase '*neatly poetise*' in the 'Second Nymphal,' p. 166, l. 16. *Cf.* also *Barons' Wars*,

iii. 39. 'In my verse, transparent, *neat* and clear.'

p. 122, l. 1. *Samuel Daniel.* In his Matilda (1594), Drayton had been much more complimentary :—

"Fair Rosamond, of all so highly graced
Recorded in the lasting book of fame,

And in our Sainted Legendary placed
By him who strives to stellify her name ;
Yet will some matrons say she was to blame :
Though all the world bewitched with his rime,
Yet all his skill cannot excuse her crime."

And so, too, at the end of his *Endimion and Phœbe* (1595) he apologises to him, next after Spenser, thus :

" And thou, the sweet Musæus of these times,
Pardon my rugged and unfiled rimes,
Whose scarce invention is too mean and base
When Delia's glorious Muse doth come in place."

In a prefatory sonnet to his *Idea* (1605) he says :

"Many there be excelling in this kind,
Whose well trick'd rimes with all invention swell:
Let each commend, as best shall like his mind,
Some *Sidney, Constable,* some *Daniel.*
That thus their names familiarly I sing,
Let none think them disparaged to be;
Poor men with reverence may speak of a King,
And so may these be spoken of by me."

I suspect, too, that Daniel is the Melibœus of the Sixth Eclogue :

" Thou that down from the goodly Western waste
To drink at Avon driv'st thy sunned sheep,
Good Melibœus, that so wisely hast
Guided the flocks delivered thee to keep."

Daniel's Delia dwelt by the Avon.

p. 123, l. 10. *Alexander*, Sir William, of Menstry, Earl of Stirling, the friend of Drummond of Hawthornden, and author of a portentous epic called 'Doomsday.'

p. 127, l. 7. *Hays*, country dances.

p. 128, l. 7. *and.* Drayton frequently misplaces this conjunction for metrical reasons ; see p. 134, l. 20 ; p. 137, l. 5 ; perhaps most curious of all, p. 145, l. 6.

Notes

p. 129, l. 1. *when.* Drayton not uncommonly uses the relative for the demonstrative; see p. 135, l. 25; p. 145, l. 1.

p. 134, l. 25. *lin,* cease.

p. 138, l. 10. *lubrican* "it seems was a spirit, but of his properties we are not fully informed."—Nares.

p. 152, l. 7. *Trenchmore,* "a boisterous sort of dance to a lively tune in triple time."—Halliwell.

l. 14. *ging,* company.

p. 167, l. 33. *notted,* without horns.

p. 176, l. 15. Something is wrong with this line. Perhaps we should read '*the* only music'; but what does 'this world' mean? The world of waters?

p. 178, l. 9. *lyam,* a leash.

l. 11. *my gaffle on my rack.* This is Nares' correction for '*or* my rack,' the gaffle being the steel lever for bending the cross-bow.

l. 18, *earning,* same word as 'yearning.'

p. 179, l. 6. *Matachynes,* a Spanish dance with swords. Nares says that Drayton, by calling them 'wanton,' mistook their nature.

p. 183, l. 23. *cullings,* the residue.

p. 184, l. 6. *flawns,* custards.

l. 7. *whig,* a thin liquor made from whey.

l. 13. *sleeve,* silk.

www.ingramcontent.com/pod-product-compliance
Lightning Source LLC
Chambersburg PA
CBHW031811230426
43669CB00009B/1099